A Listening Ear

Reflections on Christian Caring

PAUL TOURNIER

Texts selected by Charles Piguet

Translated by Edwin Hudson

AUGSBURG Publishing House • Minneapolis

A LISTENING EAR
Reflections on Christian Caring

First published 1984 by Editions de Caux under the title *Vivre à l'écoute*. First American edition 1987 Augsburg Publishing House.

Original French edition copyright © 1984 Editions de Caux. This English translation copyright © 1986 by Hodder and Stoughton.

Library of Congress Cataloging-in-Publication Data

Tournier, Paul.
    A listening ear.

    Translation of: Vivre à l'écoute.
    Bibliography: p.
    1. Caring—Religious aspects—Christianity.   2. Interpersonal rela-
tions—Religious aspects—Christianity.   3. Medicine—Religious aspects—
Christianity.   4. Life.   I. Piguet, Charles.   II. Title.
BV4647.S9T6713   1987   248   87-1412
ISBN 0-8066-2266-0

Manufactured in the U.S.A.   APH 10-3900

        4   5   6   7   8   9   0   1   2   3   4   5   6   7   8   9

Also by Paul Tournier:

ESCAPE FROM LONELINESS
THE GIFT OF FEELING
GUILT AND GRACE
THE HEALING OF PERSONS
LEARN TO GROW OLD
THE MEANING OF GIFTS
THE MEANING OF PERSONS
THE PERSON REBORN
THE STRONG AND THE WEAK
TO UNDERSTAND EACH OTHER
THE VIOLENCE WITHIN
THE WHOLE PERSON IN A BROKEN WORLD

CONTENTS

FOREWORD

The Geneva ring road is fast, and it takes me only about twenty minutes to drive from the United Nations quarter to the charming village of Troinex, a complete contrast with the big city. It is a glorious June day, and I find Paul Tournier sitting waiting for me in the shade of a tall pine tree.

It is a very different scene from when I first came here, barely four months ago, to talk about this book. The garden paths were covered in snow, and after a discussion in the doctor's study, he came out to see me off and to wish me good luck in the task I had undertaken, along lines which he had suggested.

I was impressed by his vitality. He had come out without an overcoat in mid-February, and when I begged him to go back in so as not to catch cold, this octogenarian had answered, "It's just a matter of habit and of training the body, you know. All you have to do is not to start wearing an overcoat in September."

But today the sun is shining, and it is pleasantly warm. A squirrel runs across the lawn a few feet away from us.

"Dr. Tournier, I must tell you that I got a lot out of studying and going through those texts of yours."

"Really?"

"It took me back to my own commitment to my vocation, a long time ago. It is so easy to allow activity to crowd out real care for others. One is always in a rush, and one stops listening to other people. I've pulled myself up short several times these last few weeks, and I think you have something to do with it."

We look over the passages we have in mind. The sheaf that we have garnered during the last few months has turned out to be much more abundant and varied than we imagined when we first discussed the project. From various sources have come chapters contributed by the doctor to books published in English or German, radio interviews, and unpublished recordings of lectures which have been circulating almost in secret.

We discuss details of editing, publication, and author's rights. As all those who meet Paul Tournier discover, seemingly ordinary conversations lead to the most intense contact. For a long time we remain silent; a silence in which our hearts are full. At last he stands up. He hurries into the house and comes back holding in his hand a photomontage of the covers of all his books, published in nineteen different languages.

"I came across it again going through some papers . . ."

I get into my car and start the engine. Paul trots along in front of the car down to the end of the drive, where it opens on to a bend in the road. He looks left and right, and then with a great swing of his arm waves me on: "Go on, the road is clear."

For Paul Tournier accompanying people is not just theoretical.

CHARLES PIGUET

One

WHY I WRITE

Preface to an anthology of selected passages published in
German in 1980

At first I declined to write this introduction, because at the time I was consumed with anxiety over a projected lecture tour in South Africa—and anyway it is quite distasteful to write a preface to one's own work!

But perhaps it is an opportunity to ask myself why it is that I write at all. I was struck by a remark made by Anais Nin, an American writer born in Paris, who asks herself this question in her book *In Favour of the Sensitive Man and other Essays* (W. H. Allen, 1978), and answers, "One writes because one has to create a world in which one can live." Well, that is why I write also. A world in which one could live would be, I think, one in which there was real contact between people, in which we could be completely open with one another, and so help each other to become genuinely ourselves.

I write in order to share with my readers the privilege I have had of becoming, without seeking it or expecting it, the intimate confidant of so many men and women of all ages and conditions, people who have come to me determined for once in their lives to speak the truth about themselves, instead of constantly having to weigh up what they should or should not be saying.

I have heard many a one say with a sigh and a wonderful smile, after a difficult confession, "What a relief it is to be able to say it all at last!" All? Of course one can never say everything. But there are some emotions, pent up and unexpressed, which block the flow of life. It is not only a matter of admitting to things we are ashamed of; often it may involve telling of an exceptional personal experience, in which all at once we have glimpsed something very real and precious, some deep belief which gives meaning to the whole of life.

It is rare for people to open their hearts to each other in this way, even in the case of married couples, or close friends. When I question the person who has just told me something he has never dared to admit to anyone else, he replies: "I was afraid of not being understood." That is it: he has felt he was understood. The feeling that he is understood is what helps him to live, to face any problem, however difficult, without being false to himself. It is a moment of truth, of confidence, of deep emotion, for him—but also for me! I have not understood only with my head, but with my heart. I too will never be the same again. The mysterious resonance we have experienced is personal contact, which commits each of us to the other.

Then, quite often, the same thought occurs to us both: Ought not this to be the normal, universal, relationship between people? Even though it is so rare. Even though, as Dr. Jean de Rougemont says, human beings constantly seek each other and at the same time flee from each other.

I have been able to measure the solitude of modern people. True dialog is very rare—in conversations each follows his or her own line; ideas pass each other by without meeting. In his fine book on "discovering oneself" *(Découverte de soi)* the philosopher Georges Gusdorf remarks that one can count on the fingers of one hand the "privileged moments" in most people's lives—those fleeting instants which determine the direction of a person's life for decades.

Gusdorf points out that these moments always involve an encounter. A genuine dialog, a film, a show, a sermon, an unforgettable moment of musical enchantment or of the contemplation of nature, a book—each is an encounter. We always seek the person behind the ideas which an author deploys. His ideas may be interesting or debatable, but all at once we come upon some remark which touches us personally. That encounter is the vital thing. I am struck by this when I meet unknown readers in some distant country. They refer to something I have written, sometimes only a passing remark to which I have attached no particular importance at the time, and yet it has been sufficient to establish a lasting bond between them and me.

So that is the justification for a book such as this one. Perhaps the readers will pick up some remark which will help them to live, to feel that I understand what is stirring in their hearts. For men and women are lonely in their search for the heart of the matter, for personal contact.

Two

THE POWER OF LISTENING AND THE POWER OF SILENCE

Interview published in the monthly magazine *Changer*, February 1984

Doctors are among the busiest people in our day. It is significant, therefore, that it is a doctor who emphasizes for us the importance of silence, of meditation. You have practiced meditation constantly for the last fifty years. Why?

Modern people lack silence. They no longer lead their own lives; they are dragged along by events. It is a race against the clock. I think that what so many people come to see me for is to find a quiet, peaceful person who knows how to listen and who isn't thinking all the time about what he has to do next. If your life is chock-full already, there won't be room for anything else. Even God can't get anything else in. So it becomes essential to cut something out. I'm putting it as simply as I can.

Can one define silence?

It is extremely difficult. For me, above all it is a waiting. I wait for God to stimulate my thoughts sufficiently to renew me, to make me creative instead of being what St. Paul calls a tinkling cymbal. It's the cornerstone of my life. It is an attempt at seeing people and their problems from God's point of view, insofar as that is possible.

What was your first experience of meditation?

Trying to listen to God for a whole hour and hearing nothing at all!

Others would have been put off. You weren't?

It put me on my mettle! Was I really not capable of doing something so simple? What had interested me was the idea of listening in to God. That goes beyond silence. Silence is no longer an end, but a means. The most precious thing of all is the possibility of being, through the words in my mind or through my inborn unconscious faculties, the recipient of thoughts that come from God.

After that first failure, or that first challenge, did you persevere?

Often after that my meditations seemed pretty unproductive. There comes into one's mind the thought of some step to take, perhaps a letter to write. We have to realize that we always resist doing quite simple things that we know we ought to do. If we can manage to understand the reason for this resistance we are on the way to self-discovery. That's what makes meditation precious.

There's a resemblance here to psychoanalysis. Who was it who established the value of silence?

Freud. He revealed its enormous power. Under psychoanalysis, there is a moment when the subject feels silence weighing on him terribly. He longs for the doctor to say something to him. Silence has the power to force you to dig deep inside yourself. It was a phenomenon well known to Jesus, who would go off to spend a whole night in the desert. St. Paul was aware of it, and all the mystics as well. It involves a restructuring of the person, which leads to the discovery of underlying motives.

Can silence be an important element in the life of a nonbeliever?

Of course. Silence has a psychological aspect. For me it means listening to God, but for others it may represent a way of deepening self-knowledge.

I have often had occasion to share silence with others. I can say in general that it is the less sophisticated person who understands best. A rustic who decides to listen in to God can in five minutes make you a list of all his problems, which a professor of philosophy would be incapable of doing. Children understand straight away, too. The naked truth comes out. We are dealing with simple matters, and modern people have lost their understanding of such things.

So that intellectualism can, in a way, be a hindrance?

Yes, indeed. In medical practice too it is the intellectual who is the most difficult to treat. Not for nothing did Jesus say that we must become like little children. On the other hand, an intellectual who undergoes a profound spiritual experience has much that he or she can offer.

You said in a recent lecture that meditation had helped you to discover "the immensity of the personal problems" that almost everyone has to face. How did you come to this perception?

People confide their problems to us in accordance with our readiness to listen. It is a barometer. The ability to offer oneself depends to a great extent on this discipline of meditation in which we bring our human relationships before God in order to smooth the way.

You spoke just now of meditation practiced in the company of others. Is there not a danger there of imposing your thoughts on others?

The more I am persuaded of the importance of seeking God's will for oneself, the more skeptical I become about the possibility of saying what is his will for others. That is the source of all kinds of intolerance and abuse. People who claim to know what is God's will try to impose it upon others with the arrogance which comes from the conviction that they are the repositories of divine truth. I avoid that at all costs. I can never know what is God's will for someone else. Even in psychoanalysis doctors generally prefer that their patients should make their own discoveries. If doctors start making suggestions of their own, they almost always go astray.

If it is wrong to tell others what they ought to do, do you still think that one can help them to overcome their mental blockages?

It is only insofar as I can overcome my own reluctance to recognize the truth about myself, that I can help others to overcome their own resistance.

I ought to say a little about the role of silence in the marriage relationship. For my wife and me it was essential. It is in silence that one thinks of the things that are not easy to say to each other, and which one is afraid may be misunderstood or arouse criticism. In silence, these restraints lose their force. Without these periods of silence we tend to confess only the favorable things and not the things we are ashamed of. For us, meditation became the road to really knowing each other. Many couples who think they are talking openly to one another about everything are just deluding themselves. You can even say prayers and sing hymns together and still have mental reservations and no true openness towards one another. In meditation there takes place a reciprocal interpenetration which cannot be achieved by any other means.

The morning quiet time seems so difficult at first. Can one get used to it so that it comes naturally?

Quite often I have persevered with it just in order to stick to a resolution I have made. Obviously there are times when you are more or less forcing yourself to do it for the sake of your own self-esteem. You get through periods of spiritual drought that way. And then the thing becomes real again; you get a fresh start, as it were, and you don't any longer have to rely on the motivation of vanity.

We know you don't like laying down rules, but can you give some indication of what a typical meditation might consist of?

I practice written meditation. It may not suit everybody. There are some who say that having a pencil in their hand is enough to prevent them meditating, because they feel that it makes it too mechanical. But it suits me very well, because I used to have a tendency to day-dream in my meditation. The act of writing prevents me from slipping into wool gathering. Aimless musing may be agreeable, but it has nothing to do with the realities of life. Another thing is that writing things down is like knocking nails in to make them firmer. It commits us more.

Do you consciously direct your thoughts?

As little as possible. God's way of thinking is different from ours. And the whole point is that we should take the great leap from our own thoughts to those of God.

One last point. How are we to discern God's will amongst the clutter of our own imaginings?

The most important thing is patience. If I may recount a personal experience, I must tell you that I once almost gave up medicine in order to become an evangelist. The idea tempted me, but my wife was not in agreement. You can see that it is not easy to be sure what is God's will. We spent some months in great perplexity, and I was even in despair at times, until I became convinced that I ought not to leave medicine, but instead introduce into medicine the experience I had had. Suddenly it all became clear: it was not a compromise, but a synthesis. That was what made it creative. It was not that the view of the one or the other had triumphed, but that a third way, a most productive one, had been found. I am happy to speak of this, because it illustrates both the importance of trying to let God guide us, and the difficulties that that involves. Patience is vital. Generally when God's will is made manifest, it is obvious and everyone recognizes it. Unfortunately, however, that is infrequent. One would like it to happen more often. But then, that would make us arrogant. . . .

Three

OVERVIEW

Extracts from an encounter with young people and a
recorded conversation, 1981

What counts most for me is encounter. Encountering
other people, a particular person, an idea, nature—encountering God, who is hidden behind all these other
encounters. The Alsatian philosopher Gusdorf once said
that when in old age one reflects upon one's life, one
perceives that there have been certain privileged moments, and that they have all resulted from an encounter. His precursor Charles Secrétan, who came from the
Swiss canton of Vaud, tells of how his whole philosophy
was formed in a moment when he was contemplating
the view from the terrace outside the church at Montreux.

In my case also, encounters have been responsible for
new departures in my life. My father was a pastor and
a poet. He was seventy years old when I was born, and
he died two months after my birth. I was left with an
elder sister and my mother, but the latter died when I
was six. I became withdrawn and turned in upon myself,
a shy little boy. Seeing me today, people imagine that
giving lectures and making contact with everybody
comes naturally to me. It is the opposite of the truth. I
was the most inhibited and abnormal of children, incapable of relating to anyone, making almost as little

mark as a passing shadow. If I joined a group of people talking together, a sort of uneasy silence fell. My childhood was one of typical spiritual loneliness, in which I felt that I did not count. Since then I have met plenty of people who have the same feeling that they do not exist, or do not appear to exist.

When I was sixteen, one of my teachers must have guessed that this odd young boy needed someone to hold out a friendly hand to him, and he made a quite unprecedented gesture. He invited me to his home. That was my first encounter. I was embarrassed and overawed as I went into his small study, its walls covered with bookshelves from floor to ceiling. I did not know what to say. Later on I realized that in all probability he did not know what to say either, but he did something vitally important for me. Through him I began to exist. I was no longer a pupil in front of a teacher, but a person in front of a person. Normally in our lives each one of us plays a role which sets up certain functional relationships. What I call a personal relationship is one in which our role is not that of patient or doctor, pupil or teacher, but that of a person.

My teacher and I formed such a close relationship that I went on visiting him every week for several years. The first invitation my wife and I received after our marriage was to his house. As a teacher of Greek, philosophy was his life, and we spent a lot of time in intellectual discussions. Quite suddenly I discovered that I could take part in society with ideas of my own, and I became a debater. When I got to university I founded the General Association of Students; I became central president of the Students' Union at Zofingen. As a representative of the Red Cross I repatriated Russian prisoners-of-war. I started a "back to Calvin" movement, which brought about more storms than peace in the church in Geneva.

Nevertheless, in my heart I knew that I was missing something. A transformation, a new departure, an encounter had opened my life to the world of ideas, but the result was nothing very constructive. At that point my second encounter occurred.

In the spring of 1932 the Disarmament Conference was taking place in Geneva. At the time I was secretary of the Geneva Consistory of the Reformed Church, and I received a request from Frank Buchman[1] to be allowed to use St. Peter's Cathedral for a service for the conference delegates. His letter was accompanied by a recommendation from my friend Pastor Jean de Saussure. I consulted the Consistory chairman, and said to him, "I think they are Americans, but since Saussure recommends them, we can allow them to use the cathedral without question." So I allowed these strangers to use the cathedral, but I did not go to their service, and never dreamed that I was myself going to be profoundly affected by their action.

During the summer holiday Dr. Henri Mentha and I did a locum for each other, and I went to see one of his patients in the gynecological unit at Malagnou. It was the wife of a German journalist accredited to the League of Nations. On arriving I asked for the number of the room I wanted. The receptionist replied, "Oh! You're going to see the baroness? You won't find her an easy person to deal with." True enough! As I left, I remarked to the receptionist, "I hardly needed your warning—I could see at once that she is a shockingly difficult person." She treated her husband like a servant; she was capricious, selfish in the extreme.

One day in the autumn Mentha said to me:

"You remember the baroness?"

"Ah!" I replied, "How could I forget?"

"Well, you know, she's changed."

"It's not possible."

"It is. She came back to see me about one of her house-maids. She was very concerned about her. It's incredible."

Henri Mentha and I were members of a group he had formed seven years before, called "The worried sons of the church." The group consisted of both lay people and pastors who were working for a new awakening in the church. Mentha asked me, "Don't you think she ought to be asked what has happened to her?" A few days later he brought me the confirmation: the baroness had taken part with her husband in a meeting at Ermatingen in the canton of Thurgau, and she had changed her life, as she herself had expressed it. Clearly the matter deserved to be looked into, and I asked if we might not ask the baroness to take us to meet these people. "It seems to be something like a Salvation Army for the well-to-do," my colleague remarked.

The baroness was willing to organize a meeting, but it was for us to fix the venue. The "worried sons" often met at the house of Maître Henri Necker, a descendant of the famous banker.[2] He was a charming and very devout man. He had a magnificent mansion alongside that of the French Ambassador. It was very sumptuous, and full of old portraits. The meeting was arranged for 23 November 1932. We had invited the "worried sons" group, and a few older people connected with it whom we used to call the "worried uncles," but we had no idea who else was going to be there.

Three professors had come specially from Zurich—Thêophile Spoerri the historian, the theologian Emil Brunner, and the psychiatrist Alphonse Maeder. There was also a senior official from the League of Nations, called Jan de Bordes, who had the oversight of Austrian financial affairs. As experts in the reform of the church, we wanted to learn from them, and we asked, "What are your methods? What results do you achieve?" I was most disappointed with their answers, and I said to them, "We asked for bread, and you bring us stones." They had no method, and as for results, these consisted only of revelations about overdue taxes and other trivialities of that sort.

All the same, Jan de Bordes had spoken about meditation, and after the meeting I went up to him and asked how much time he devoted to it each day.

"That depends," he replied.

"I am asking for a precise answer."

"Well, on average one hour. Sometimes more."

Next morning I rose quietly an hour earlier than usual, being careful not to disturb my wife, and went into my study. Placing my watch on the table, I said to myself, "I am going to meditate for one hour and see what happens." I looked at my watch from time to time, and when the hour was up, I realized that I had heard nothing. Then, as I replaced my watch on my wrist I thought, "I must persevere." And at once I recognized that that very thought could well have come from God. So I persevered.

In this way I was introduced into a movement which had taken root in Geneva's international circles, and which was based on the simple idea that the problems of the world are in fact personal problems. I was fond of discussing great problems, but Jan de Bordes, League of Nations official as he was, led me to an examination of myself. I was taking part in church affairs, but had no personal experience of God. De Bordes too, like all his Dutch fellow countrymen, had been brought up as a Christian, but he had experienced a crisis. He invited me to his house, and talked to me in a personal way, not about Plato and other philosophers, but about how he had passed from Christian faith by association to Christian faith by conviction. In answer to God's call he had taken quite concrete measures to clean up the disorder of his life. What could I say in reply? I must needs talk about myself, and for the first time, at the age of thirty-two, I shed the tears of my distress as an orphan which I had been keeping back since my childhood.

The breath of the Holy Spirit blew like a wind over Geneva at that time, and many were stirred by it. It had considerable influence within the church, where, for example, instead of continuous talking, periods of silence were introduced, under the influence of the Group.

I recall a gentleman named Maurice Thudichum. With the cooperation of the "worried sons" we had organized Thursday services in the cathedral for people who used to go off skiing on Sundays. This had aroused a storm of criticism on the grounds that we were destroying the unity of Sunday worship. I went to see Thudichum, who was president of the ski club, to request his signature on an appeal for attendance at the services. He replied, "How do you expect me to sign, when I don't believe in anything?" Years later I saw this same Maurice Thudichum stand up in a rally in Vevey and declare, "I understand! I must sign a blank contract with God, and he will write in it what he will." That is commitment. Later, Thudichum took on the task of recording the names of those who had perished in the gas-chambers of the Second World War.

There was also Professor Gampert, of the Faculty of Theology. During the Disarmament Conference, Frank Buchman went to see Gampert. The professor told me afterwards that Buchman had suggested that they should meditate together. "I had always thought that meditating meant shutting one's eyes and remaining quite silent," said Gampert, "but I saw that he had his eyes open and was writing all the time. Then it was suggested to me that I should invite a few people to my house. I was pleased, and expected to be asked to say a short prayer at the end, but no! No one asked me anything."

Gampert confided this to me with the irony of the professional theologian. But he changed. I saw him again shortly before his death. A little while previously he had gone into the cathedral pulpit to bear witness to his changed life: "I was the prodigal son's elder brother," he said. I think that was the last sermon he preached.

In 1937 I experienced another new departure. At a rally in Oxford I heard Frank Buchman declare that we must apply in our public lives the personal commitments of our private lives. That determined me to devote myself to the effect on health of a person's spiritual and moral life. I started by talking it over with some of my colleagues. I went to see Schlemmer[3] in the Mont d'Or hills, and we spent a whole afternoon together in the crater of an extinct volcano. Schlemmer said to me, "Look, why don't you read Carton[4] and try? It was Carton who turned me away from narrow specialism towards an understanding of the whole person." Schlemmer talked a lot to me about Carton, who had been a lifesaver for him. While a student he had been shocked by the vulgarity and the contemptuous attitude to patients which prevailed among hospital staffs. He was contemplating giving up when he met Carton, who restored his faith in medicine. At that time I was myself attracted to Carton's ideas: the classification of temperaments and typology, notions which I have largely reconsidered since then. Carton was a theist. He conceived of God as a legislator, and of life as governed by laws which could not be disobeyed with impunity. His God was the lawgiver, rather than the God who meets us and enters into dialog with us, person to person.

In 1940 I wrote *Médecine de la personne*.[5] I submitted the manuscript to six friends, and we met in Berne to discuss it. It was a first draft, and probably made rather heavy reading. Mentha had worked like a Trojan on it, noting all the pages on which he recommended changing this and adding that. He had done a marvelously meticulous job, but I found it discouraging. Maeder, for his part, suggested that I have the first chapter published in a medical journal. "If you find that it arouses interest," he said, "you publish the second chapter." Which was as much as to say, "It won't do as a book." I spent the next few months in despair. I could see that there were too many gaps in my book for me to publish it as it was. On the other hand, if I took on board all the suggestions that had been made, it would no longer be my book. I got into such a state that Nelly went to see a close friend and said to her, "What is to be done with Paul? He's quite disheartened. He feels that he has been directed to get it published, but he's come to an impasse." Her friend's reply was, "Leave it to God." At that point the order for general mobilization was issued, and I had to join up. During my off-duty hours in the army I was able to take up my pen and start writing again. In fact I rewrote the book from beginning to end.

It seems that Maxence van der Meersch read *Médecine de la personne*. He had been denouncing the triviality of much that goes on in the medical profession, its backstairs rivalries, its mercenary patronage. He is reported to have said that had he read my book before writing his *Corps et âmes*,[6] he would not have written it in the way he did. Unfortunately I never met van der Meersch.

Now, forty years later, my books have been translated into a score of languages. I have visited Japan, to deliver twenty-five lectures. Mention of Japan reminds me of the last war, of the attack on Pearl Harbor which brought in the United States, and of the atomic bomb which ended the war. Dared one speak of these things in Japan? As there are not many people who know French there, university lecturers in French had been asked to serve as my interpreters. But I did not dare to touch on the war, for fear of causing offense. Halfway through my tour, when I had already given a dozen lectures, a big reception was held in my honor, with grand speeches, to which my reply was so perfunctory and academic that it made me sick at heart. That night God woke me and said to me, "My dear man, what on earth are you doing? You come to Japan to talk about personal relationships, and yet you conceal the thought that is uppermost in your mind. You are betraying your message."

On the following day my interpreter was a Buddhist lady, a specialist in medieval French. We went together to see the great Buddha at Nara. After spending some time in silence before the statue we went for a short walk. I said to myself, "Now, I've just got to sort this out. I am going to ask this Buddhist for some advice—advice that will come from God." Buddhists believe in the existence of God. In no way is he the monopoly of Christians. So I suggested that we should sit on a low wall at the side of the path, and meditate together in silence. I told her of the problem that was troubling me: "Ought I to talk about sensitive subjects such as the attack on Pearl Harbor and the Japanese defeat?" We spent a quarter of an hour in silence, after which I asked the young woman what she was thinking. She replied, "The war, the defeat, the atomic bomb—everyone thinks about them but nobody talks about them. If you speak in love about these things, it will be well received." That evening I was speaking in Kobe, in a packed theatre.

There were people sitting on the stairs, squatting in every available space. And at last I talked about Pearl Harbor, about the defeat, and about the memorable statement of Emperor Hirohito when he announced the surrender: "We must now accept the unacceptable, and surmount the insurmountable." You could have heard a pin drop. Contact was established.

I have no wish to belittle the intellectual training which my classics master had given me, since in introducing me to the objective, scientific side of life he had helped me to become a person. But he had never told me that he was divorced, and that his daughter by his first wife had not accepted her stepmother. I learned this from someone else. For my part, I had never talked to him about my life as an orphan. In order to cross that threshold we had to enter into a new relationship as persons. Years passed, during which I hardly ever saw him. Then I began writing. With a first book one is at a loss to know whether it is worth trying to get it published or not. I wondered to whom I might show my manuscript to see if the writing was good enough to get my message across to people. I went to see my old teacher, and found myself once more in the study into which I had made such an emotional entry so many years before. I began reading my manuscript to him. At the end of the first chapter I asked:

"Shall I go on?"

"Go on, Paul."

I read another chapter. Silence.

"Go on, Paul."

Silence once more. My anxiety was growing. Did he disapprove? Suddenly he said to me:

"Paul, we must pray together."

I knew that formerly he had been a spiritualist, believing in an impersonal spirit, and I asked him:

"Are you a Christian?"

"Yes."

"Since when?"

"Since now."

That was the supreme encounter, and we prayed together.

All over the world we meet people who have been stimulated in the same way. They have each found their own route, but they all belong to the same revolution. You can recognize them at once because they talk of the reality of life, not just theories. Their tone is personal.

Four

TAKING PERSONAL PROBLEMS INTO ACCOUNT

A talk given at Caux in 1982

I find it quite moving to be once again in this place, which holds so many memories for me, and to see familiar, friendly faces. And so I am grateful to Dr. Marc-André Jaccottet for the invitation. I did enormously appreciate his book *L'horizontal et le vertical dans la pratique médicale* (Editions de Caux).

Looking back over the years, I have to make this evening one of homage to Frank Buchman. I was very fond of Frank Buchman, and I am indebted to him for everything—everything in the spiritual adventure of my life. To Frank Buchman, to the world movement which he created, I owe my own transformation, and the transformation of our married life and our family life. To him also I owe my whole career, the new orientation in the understanding of medicine which I have been able to develop. It was indeed to him that I dedicated my first book, *Médecine de la personne.*

Stephen Foot[1] had informed me that a British publisher was prepared to take the book on one condition, namely that I withdraw the dedication to Frank Buchman. I refused. One does not withdraw a dedication which is really an expression of gratitude. I still have that sense of gratitude.

God inspired Frank Buchman, and it is through him, through his friends and fellow workers, and now through all of you, that my life has in large measure borne fruit, and that I have been able to make that voice heard within the medical profession, beyond the bounds of strictly religious gatherings.

I have been practicing in Geneva for nearly sixty years. In the spring of 1932 Frank Buchman came to Geneva from the League of Nations Disarmament Conference. It was then that I had my first experience of meditation. For fifty years now I have carried my meditation notebook in my pocket. I do not claim never to have missed a single day. I often missed, especially at first. Since my wife's death eight years ago I have never missed a day. That is the basis of my life and of everything that has come out of it. Those who have thanked me for my books know well that I have lived a life of meditation and of ministry, of personal encounters. People have opened their hearts to me, and have thus revealed to me the immensity of the problems that exist in the lives of all of us. I remember saying to myself once, "It is terrible; there are in fact secrets, terrible burdens, in the life of every man and woman. We doctors examine, observe, and make a medical diagnosis, but there is another diagnosis to be made." I began to appreciate the importance of all these problems for a person's health. Sickness comes much less often by chance than we suspect. Often it may be years before it manifests itself. There is a connection between health and all these problems which people carry about with them, and for which they seek help without knowing where to look for a solution.

I see that my old comrade Dr. Jaccottet Sr. is with us.

He and I were in the same year at medical school. One day I took him to the hill country of the Saléve, where we had a farm. When we got there he said, "I see that there are some eggs in the hen house. Let's take a little walk and collect some mushrooms, and we can make a mushroom omelette." "That will take some time!" I said to myself. But I was wrong. He picked up a basket and off we went. As we walked he was constantly bending down, picking, bending down, picking. . . . He was the son of a food inspector, and like his father knew all about mushrooms. I was astonished; in ten minutes the basket was full. I kept searching, but saw nothing but grass. I realized then how true it is that one sees only what one is prepared to see. There were mushrooms all around us, but I simply couldn't see them. That is true of human lives also: they are full of problems, and we can't see them. In our medical schools we study pathological anatomy, physiology, symptomatology, and psychology. We are well grounded in the whole of medical science, but nobody teaches us to recognize personal problems.

The world over, there are thousands and thousands of doctors who see only the scientific object—that is necessary, of course; you may be sure that I am not anti-science: quite the contrary. But it is only the visible half of the moon, the objective side. There is the other half. Many doctors have a sneaking suspicion that a large number of illnesses are the expression of some inner crisis, emotional distress, marital conflict, or failure—but how to put their finger on it? They do not know what they can do to help. And if these problems were to be laid bare, what could they say or do about them? No one has taught them how.

So what is it that helps people? Certainly not advice, for they either accept it blindly, or they reject it. In either case it does no good. What helps people is what helped me, that is to say an encounter with people who talk honestly about their own distress, their difficulties, their frustrations, their rejections, and their evasions.

The fear that doctors have of coming up against a problem to which they have no answer is a groundless one. They should understand that to help their patients to get well they have to allow them to express themselves, to reveal their feelings. Self-expression is the road to self-liberation.

I was a G.P., a family doctor. I thought I knew all about my patients; and then, all at once they began to talk to me on a deeper level. The level on which our patients are prepared to talk to us depends on the level of our own availability.

The thing that struck me straight away was that many of these problems had to do with the duality of revolt and acceptance. Suffering always evokes revolt, and the solution is always to be found in acceptance, but it is of no help to anyone to say to a person, "You must accept." What we have to do is to get doctors to understand that acceptance comes from contact with people who themselves have learned to accept. It is not a matter of logical causality, but of spiritual contact. Therefore acceptance in our patients will come from our own acceptance of our personal difficulties.

There is one doctor who has done much, far more than I have, to help the medical profession to understand the importance of personal problems: Michael Balint, a Hungarian psychoanalyst who came as a refugee to London at the time of Hitler. When I read his writings I said to myself, "That's what I have been doing for thirty years." Balint says to doctors, "You keep asking questions; the result is that all you ever get is a dossier of scientific information. Let people speak for themselves for once, let them speak freely, for an hour if necessary. It is only they who can tell you about their personal problems."

That is how I started. Again and again with patients who were just beginning to talk more freely, I had an inkling of the problem, and I would say to them, "Listen, perhaps there isn't time at the moment, with a line of people in the waiting room—come to my house this evening, and we can talk not as doctor and patient, but man to man." Later, at my fireside, the atmosphere was quite different.

There is nevertheless a very clear difference between Balint and me. Psychoanalysts remain in the domain of science; they only wish to look at problems objectively. I must admit, however, that the psychoanalysts have been very kind to me. I was invited to meet them, and they asked me: "What procedure do you adopt?"

I replied: "I don't know."

"Well, what is your method?"

"I haven't any."

That disconcerted them. What irked them was that I was violating one of the fundamental principles of psychoanalysis—the moral neutrality of the doctor. Sometimes I would talk about my own experiences, even about my faith, and that upset my colleagues, because it went against rule number one laid down by Freud and all his successors: that we must be like a screen on which our patients can project any image they wish, but the screen must be blank to start with. The psychoanalyst listens to people telling the story of their lives, he allows them to express their problems, but the one thing he must not do is to depart from his objective stance as the scientist who takes everything in, makes notes, perhaps, but says nothing.

Thus from the start there was a "Tournier problem."

Do you know who came to my defense? Professor Flournoy, who was one of the first of the Swiss psychoanalysts, following immediately upon Jung and Maeder. In an article which appeared in the *International Review of Psychology* he wrote: "Dr. Tournier is accused of failing to maintain neutrality, and even of sometimes giving expression to his personal beliefs. Let us admit that we all do so." He went on to quote Charles Odier, another psychoanalyst, who said, "Sooner or later the doctor has to come down from his scientific pedestal and become human once more." That bore witness to a breadth of mind on the part of the psychoanalysts which not all Christians have, and which I greatly appreciated.

Let us return to Balint. He remained the silent man, but he realized that doctors have so much to do, so many patients to see, that only exceptionally can they interview them at length.

I have recently read a book on which he was working before his death and which has since been published by his wife under the title *Six Minutes for the Patient*.[2] That is the way things are in England, it seems; the average time a doctor spends with each patient is six minutes.

The question raised by Balint and his wife is this: what can doctors do to arrive at a deeper level of medical practice? Curiously enough, they use a new expression: the "flash." They give no definition: the word is self-explanatory. Suddenly there is a flash, that is to say, a genuine encounter between doctor and patient. Now what can the flash be but something not rational, not scientific? An impression, a feeling which for my part I should call communion. There is indeed from time to time, sometimes without a word being said, a feeling of meeting—the flash! Balint and his wife say it is an experience you don't forget. So there they stand, on the edge of the irrational, but they fear to step across the divide, because it has always been drilled into them that they must remain objective.

With this notion of the flash Balint apprehends what is missing in medicine, something which is not scientific, an opportunity for each person to bring out his or her own problems, to try to live differently. It can happen in a second—even during a six-minute consultation. An element intervenes which escapes all objective definition, but which is always a feeling of genuine meeting. A meeting is between two, or is it three? Even with Balint there is the unseen presence of God. The flash has of itself, within itself, an element of divine reality, even when it occurs between an analyst and a patient neither of whom is a believer. "It is not those who say to me 'Lord, Lord. . . .' "

The flash is not forgotten, either by the patient or by the doctor. It is an experience, something lived. Balint of course would say that it is a psychological experience. I maintain that it is a spiritual experience. It is a moment when God speaks, and human beings are set free.

As Dr. Paul Campbell quite rightly said just now, people are afraid of emotion. Emotion—that is what the psychoanalysts find so difficult to codify. It was my problem too: I was afraid of emotion. Having been an orphan, I had always repressed my feelings and turned in upon myself. It was with Jan de Bordes, the international civil servant, that I wept for the first time over the deaths of my father and mother. A flash indeed, which liberated me from that psychological blockage.

My ambition was to be a humane doctor. I wanted to be liked. My manner towards people was pleasant, even paternalistic. That did not take me very far. If we are to go further than that we need to be freed from ourselves. I did not realize that I was myself the resistance blocking the current. Our task, then, is to help doctors to escape from their scientific prison. That does not mean that they have to stop being scientists; but they have got to understand that medicine is not only science.

Theodore Flournoy, the founder of modern science, said: "In order to practice science, it is necessary to disregard transcendence." For science, that is true. But in the practice of medicine it cannot be disregarded. The flash applies not only to the psychological nature of human beings, but also to our religious nature. I can always say to myself, "This patient is sent to me by God; he has problems—it is not I who can solve them, but God." I must make him welcome, and be ready for a person-to-person encounter. That requires the doctor to come down from his or her scientific pedestal, exactly as in the case of my evening fireside chats; or as Balint advocated, both in his extended interviews, and in his "flashes," of which several of his colleagues speak without always realizing what is involved. All things considered, they come close to personal commitment.

I hold that the flash occurs when there is reciprocity. The scientific attitude is the nonreciprocal attitude of the scholar: on one side the one who knows, and on the other the one who knows nothing. You only need to see the reaction of the average doctor when a patient tries to contradict him or her and says, "You know, Dr. So-and-so says something quite different." The doctor is furious. What we have is an asymmetrical situation in which the doctor knows, and gives the orders, while all the patient has to do is to comply. There is no flash along that road. The flash can happen only when we are freed from our claim to know more than the patient. As far as pathology is concerned, we ought to know more than the patient does, but in the matter of one's own sickness, the patient knows more about it than we do.

We are touching here on the problem of the meaning

of disease. The medical diagnosis is an objective, scientific matter. But when we come to the realm of meaning, that is for the patient to discover. The more our patients are concerned with the meaning of their sickness, the more important it is that they are able to express themselves. And to be ready not to get an answer. It is not I who can tell a patient what is the meaning of his or her illness. All I can talk about is my own search for a meaning for myself.

In order to tackle a question as difficult as that of meaning, it is important to realize that often the answer comes only afterwards. Sometimes years later a patient will say to you, "You know, thinking about those years of illness, I see now that they were bound to lead to such-and-such a result." Since it is true that the meaning of an illness is often apparent only later, it follows that an act of faith must be made at the start: we have to have faith that there is a meaning. Either nothing has meaning, or everything has. If there is a meaning for the world, there is also a meaning for each one of us. But that requires a relationship different from the objective relationship. The doctor has to perform his task as a scientist who knows what the patient does not know, but on one condition: he must accept that there is also something which the patient knows and he does not; that the problems which the patient ponders in his heart during nights of sleeplessness double, as it were, the suffering of his disease. How many people say, "What can I have done for God to do this to me?" So many sick people have come to me to talk about the problem of guilt, often of false guilt. I ask them why they don't go and talk to their own doctor about it. "Oh!" they say. "He never has the time."

Actually, time is not the problem. The problem is the need for a change on the part of the doctor. Balint himself talks about a minimal but indispensable change in the person of the doctor. He is alluding only to the openness of mind which makes us aware of personal problems. But a more profound change is called for. Doctors need not only to be observers of psychological problems, but to adopt an attitude of reciprocity which involves their being ready to open their hearts about their own problems. That is what creates the flash, the authentic relationship. It is a very difficult move for a doctor to make, more so for the male doctor than for the female doctor.

There are many doctors who sincerely seek to establish this mutual relationship. They would like to talk—to talk about the person; but you can talk about it all your life without arriving at a personal relationship. I explain to them: "You will never discover that sort of relationship until you open your own heart."

"Oh! And how do I do that?"

"Well, this evening you must talk to us about your own life."

I came back that afternoon to find my colleague sweating over a blank piece of paper.

"So, professor, it isn't going well?"

"I've nothing at all to say."

"What! You've lived forty years without anything happening?"

"Oh yes, of course, like everybody else I have the occasional cup of coffee—I mean, I've nothing to say that would be of any interest."

There's suppression for you! I try to help, and say to him:

"Didn't you lose a son at the age of twenty?"

"Oh, but that's something I can't talk about!" How afraid we are of our emotions!

Everything that I have put into my books has been learned from my patients. There are some who would take a plane to come and see me, just for the sake of experiencing personal contact before flying off once more. Such poverty, such emptiness is unbelievable. They need someone to whom they can take their personal crises, their doubts, to whom they can say everything. How many people have confided to me as they leave: "That's what I've been looking for these twenty years!" So the price that we have to pay is to be willing to forsake our scientific stance in order to establish a personal relationship. It requires a real effort.

Recently I went to visit a German colleague, Dr. Lechler, in the clinic he has founded near Karlsruhe. He worked for years in America with Alcoholics Anonymous, which is also an offshoot of Frank Buchman's movement, and then he said to himself, "There aren't only alcohol alcoholics. We are all alcoholics about something." There are sleeping-pill alcoholics, chocolate alcoholics, committee alcoholics. He tried to use the method of Alcoholics Anonymous for the purpose of liberating people for whom ill health is an expression of some kind of slavery. In his clinic even those who have been incapable of sleep without sleeping tablets for twenty years are told, "There are no medicines here." After a few days, they sleep. On condition, of course, that they are given something else. And what is that something else? It is love. I was greatly impressed. The patients have a chance to express their feelings and enter into dialog. There is a team of psychiatrists there who work extremely closely together. They meet every morning to share their ideas, and when anyone speaks in the assembly you cannot tell whether it is a doctor or a patient. There is a fraternal atmosphere, and I have never, never in my whole life, seen an assembly in which each person speaks so openly and freely in public; I myself was able simply to read out from my notebook what I had written during my morning meditation. I realized what an enormous influence one's surroundings can have. Usually people are afraid of giving offense, and so remain deep-frozen in their own permafrost. What is needed is a warm breeze, a breath of love; but where is it to come from? Lechler knows very well. Together with his eight psychiatrists he spent a whole winter in Bible study, training his team. Now he holds a Bible study session weekly. It is noncompulsory, but everyone attends, and it is the basis of the life of his clinic.

I recall too a story told me by my friend Jean de Rougemont, a surgeon in Lyon. His son died of a sarcoma after a year in a hospital. It is terrible for a surgeon to watch his own son for twelve whole months moving towards death. Then one fine day, in the very room which his son had occupied, he came upon a little old woman, inconsolable over the death of her daughter. There she was, nonplussed, bereft of the will to live, numbed. He tried to console her with kindly words, but to no avail. Could he talk to her about his son? Such things are so private. In the end he said to her, "Do you know, my son died in this room." The very next day the old woman got up, put on her best dress, a dab of powder, a little hat, and walked out into the street, alive again. My friend aptly remarked, "She was like a clock that had stopped at the time of her daughter's death."

Such dramatic incidents make up the reality of every doctor's life, far more often than you would think. There are many doctors who have themselves suffered bereavement, many who struggle to keep other people's marriages together when their own is on the rocks. We must see things as they are. There is only one solution— helping each other to recognize our problems, being sincere, being able to talk about the reality of our own lives, our own doubts, difficulties, and perplexities.

I have to admit that I am afraid of meeting the sick, just because I have no special technique. How comfortable it would be to have one! All I should have to do would be to press the starter button, so to speak. But it is in ourselves that the thing happens, and in ourselves means between God and us. It is when we are listening to God in our quiet times, difficult as that is, that we come to recognize the problems that are blocking true contact with others. The medicine of the whole person, then, is a medicine of the person of the doctor, not just of the person of the patient.

Can you envisage the possibility of a patient who has been liberated in the way you describe being enlisted to help other patients, so that the doctors' work may to a certain extent be spread?

I have practiced that on a wide scale. I have often entrusted patients to former patients, and there is nothing like it. It is people who have themselves been liberated who can liberate others. Maeder spoke of the person of the doctor as a medicine, and here we have our patients' persons themselves becoming a medicine. I have therefore used it, and it is particularly appropriate in group therapy. It really is a excellent system.

You said that men find it harder to express their inner feelings than women do. What can a woman do to help her husband to unburden himself without bossing him or giving the impression that she wants to manage everything for him?

You know how it is: a man comes home from work, his

face lined with worry. His wife throws her arms around his neck, and says:

"My dear, whatever is the matter?"

"Nothing's the matter."

After a while she says: "But, darling, one just has to look at you! Something's the matter. I married you for better or worse. I want to help you, I love you. Come on, tell me what's wrong."

"Nothing's wrong."

When they sit down to their meal the mother tells the children to be quiet. "Daddy's very tired, because he works so hard to buy all those sweets you eat."

The children are sent to bed, and then husband and wife are alone, face to face. "Now then, tell me what's gone wrong," she says.

"I told you! You're getting on my nerves with your questions. You're imagining things."

Men always say that: you're imagining things. After that, the more questions the wife asks, the more stubbornly the husband refuses to answer.

So your question is a very important one. Countless women have said to me in my consulting room: "I never manage to have any real dialog with my husband."

I see the husband and say to him: "Your wife tells me that she never manages to enter into any real dialog with you."

"What do you mean? She's crazy. We talk about everything."

That's the truth—they do talk about everything, but impersonally! We have come to the divide I was talking about. One talks about Afghanistan, the price of potatoes, monetarism, the children's careers, school reports—in fact about everything, but nothing personal.

Lots of married couples are like that. The more the wife wants to have a dialog with her husband, wants him to tell her about his fears, his hopes, his difficulties, the more silent he becomes. That is what happened with me. I was always lecturing my wife, explaining all sorts of scientific, psychological things; but I never actually listened to her.

In many marriages the wife is always talking. Some women have said to me, "I can go on talking to my husband for a whole evening without him uttering a single word in reply. He stays behind his newspaper, and when I stop every now and then to ask him if he's listening, he replies 'Mmm!' and so I just carry on."

I began really listening to my wife when we meditated together. I have always lived in the objective world of science, and since she was less of a scientist than I, I took it upon myself to educate her. She was quite a good pupil, in fact, but it never occurred to me that she might have something to teach me that I did not know. It was in meditation that I began to appreciate the importance of what she said, and also to give her an opportunity of expressing herself. That, of course, is the real answer to your question, if you can carry it out. But what you want to know is what happens when the resource of meditation is not available. In that case, I think it is difficult. Women have to realize how much they need to be led by God.

I have seen quite a lot of couples who had begun practicing meditation together, but have given up after a short while. Occasionally one or the other has continued, but they no longer do it together. I have always tried to get at the reason. It has almost always been because the wife has started giving her husband advice. You know what I mean: the husband, who is facing heavy responsibilities and complex problems at work, comes home and ventures to say a little about some trouble he has had with an employee. His wife says, "If I were in your place, I'd sack him right away." Whereupon he says no more about his troubles.

My experience as a doctor prompts me to counsel wives not to press their husbands too hard in an effort to worm their secrets out of them, but to be very conscious of the difficulties many men have to face, and if possible to take the matter to God and ask him for guidance.

I have a reputation as the man of the human person, but it was my wife who taught me respect for the person. Respect means acknowledging real equality. So that the wife brings as much that is vital to the union as the husband, and is not restricted to sewing on buttons or preparing tasty dishes. Many men treat their wives' talk as background music. People often joke about women who are always talking, but they talk because men do not listen to them. When a woman says, "My husband says . . . my son says . . . my father says . . .," she has said everything, because a woman takes seriously what a man says. The converse is much less true. I think that women's words carry less weight in society, at least on the level of serious intellectual discussion. The reason is that in men the affective side of their nature has been completely suppressed.

More and more, nowadays, we seem to want to chop time up into pieces. You spoke of six minutes per patient; my doctor gives them twenty minutes, and even that seems to be very little. Do you think that this increasing haste and the fragmentation of time are reversible?

I have made my own consultations longer and longer. I can do so because heaps of my fellow doctors are de-

lighted to have more patients, and I am in great favor
with my colleagues because I am not jealous. Old doctors who complain about the way people flock to their
younger colleagues would do well to devote a little more
time to listening to the patients they have. The real ob-
stacle lies much more in people's hearts than in their
circumstances. Circumstances are important too, of
course, but I think that those six minutes per patient are
a kind of escape. The whole system is responsible. One
can see a patient a hundred times without ever going
below the surface of things. Add all those six minutes
together, week after week—what a lot of wasted time!
One single hour of genuine deep conversation would
have got to the bottom of the problem. Take, for instance, certain gynaecological ailments: a woman may
visit the doctor every week for twenty years, when the
problem is really a marital one, which two or three hours
of genuine dialog might have served to clear up.

Sometimes the patient speaks in code. If he says,
"Well, doctor, is it serious?" he means, "Am I in danger
of dying? I should like to talk about death." The doctor's
response? "We are going to do another X-ray." It is not
my intention to poke fun at my colleagues—all sorts of
investigations are obviously necessary; but it is so much
easier to carry out an examination than to enter into
genuine dialog.

*Do all serious organic illnesses have a psychological or
spiritual basis?*

Certainly not. What I can say, however, is that in my
lifetime I have witnessed an extraordinary change. At
the time I began, attention was focused on characteristic
psychosomatic conditions such as the stomach ulcer.
Gradually attention was turned to a number of other

diseases, notably tuberculosis. I recall my astonishment the first time it was suggested to me, by an American doctor, that rheumatism had psychological causes. Then, about ten years ago, another American colleague raised with me the possibility of cancer having a psychosomatic origin.

Doctors used to reckon that psychological problems played a part in one or two percent of cases. Now one hears figures of 95% to 98%; even for quite organic diseases. We all carry microbes about inside ourselves, they say. Why are they not all active? A crisis of conscience may favor their development.

However, we must be careful not to make sweeping generalizations and say that all diseases are psychosomatic. Least of all is it true of a fracture, for instance (though one could ask, "Why did he fall?"). We must refrain from setting ourselves up as judges, laying down what is somatic and what is psychic. We must renounce the pretension of science that everything can be classified, and simply seek to help, without being too preoccupied with diagnosis. It was Jung who pointed out that in psychology the diagnosis is not basically very important.

Do you believe that the type of doctor-patient, husband-wife relationship that you have described ought to be the norm in the lives of all of us?

Yes, of course. It often happens that after a "flash" there is a marvelous moment when you look at each other, and the patient says, "What a relief it is to be able to say it all at last." Sometimes I reply, "After all, that is what life ought to be like." It is what life ought to be like at least between people who know each other, a husband and wife, for example, who have vowed to make their marriage a wonderful success. In the flash we have a sort of presentiment of what human life truly ought to be. It is a foretaste given us from time to time, given us in perhaps only one or two privileged moments in a whole lifetime, but our lives are never the same again—they are, as we say, changed.

It seems that the younger generation is very susceptible to psychological disorders. The other day I met a young person who told me, "I am quite proud of being a depressive." Is it one of the ills of modern society which actually brings people to the point of taking pride in being sick?

People take pride in what they can. The pupil who cannot be top of the class will willingly opt for the bottom, because that way he isn't just a nobody! Everybody has some pride; it comes into everything. But I think that young people today are the victims of our modern society, which, because of its formalism, creates a climate that favors the ills we are speaking of. The number of neuroses seems to me—and to many doctors—to be symptomatic of the ills of society. These are questions about which one can go on arguing endlessly. The important thing is that the only way to heal society is to heal men and women one by one.

Behind the rather academic arguments about the evolution of civilization lies a simpler problem, that of knowing how to talk to people as individuals. What strikes me in quite a lot of my recent contacts with young people is that there are all sorts among them, but that most of them have a deep desire to live meaningful lives.

Can you say something about the support of patients suffering from an incurable disease?

There has been a complete turnaround in this domain, thanks to a woman by the name of Elisabeth Kübler-Ross. People in the United States are even more afraid of death than people in Europe, and it was she, actually in the United States, who drew attention to the cowardice of leaving patients alone with their fears, because of one's own fear of emotion. Not long ago I met Mme Kübler-Ross in Basle, where she was attending a dinner. (She was born in Langenthal, south of Basle.) She said to me, "You are in every one of my lectures." I replied, "And you in mine." We kissed each other.

She first had to overcome her own fear of emotion. Some theology students had asked her to help in preparing a study on the subject of people's state of mind on the approach of death. She had to admit that no one knew anything about it because no one talked to dying people about death. So she asked at her hospital to see a dying person.

"And what do you want to do with the dying person?"

"Talk to him."

"About what?"

"His death."

"You must be mad!"

That woman caused a revolution, and not only in the United States. That was some years ago, but even in Switzerland our hospitals now organize support for the dying.

Again and again doctors have confessed to me how they have spaced out their visits to patients when there was nothing more they could do for them. Surgeons in particular are apt to feel an acute sense of guilt when they have tried hard to save a life, and then realize there is nothing more they can do. We need to understand them, and avoid judging and criticizing them. It is a fact

that the subtleties of the unconscious often find for us
a way of avoiding having to face up to the great existential problems of life.

Five

THE THIRD DIMENSION OF MEDICINE

Talk at the World Council of Churches, 1978

As a committed Christian I have always aimed at bringing my beliefs into my work; but it was only in the middle of my life, some forty years ago, that I began to discover how to do so. I had begun writing books, and various colleagues expressed to me their desire to unite faith and medicine. It is not an easy union to bring about. We talk religion in religious gatherings, and then carry on with our work in the way we were taught at medical school.

A year ago I was in Japan on a lecture tour. One of my engagements was in Kyoto, under the chairmanship of Professor Ohashi. The following morning my colleagues came to the hotel to take me to see some Buddhist temples. The first to arrive was Professor Kuma, of Kobe. We chatted for a moment, and then he told me the following story:

"My father was a doctor before me, and a very well-known one. So I worked hard to achieve a reputation on my own account. I built a large clinic, and ten years ago I was able to say to myself: 'Well, I have succeeded.'

"At the same time doubts began to creep in, as if the adventure of my life was over, and I was falling into a

51

routine. I talked with Professor Ohashi about it, and he said to me: 'Go and spend some time at the Jung Institute in Zurich. It will broaden your outlook.'

"That was what I did, and I found myself at the start of a new adventure. I was discovering the second dimension of medicine. It was not that I had become a psychotherapist, but I realized that in all my patients there were psychological factors at work, and that there was an interplay between the classical disease and these factors. Then, two years ago, Professor Ohashi said to me: 'You ought to read Tournier.'

"I read all your books that have appeared in Japanese so far, and I discovered the third dimension of medicine. I don't mean that I became a Buddhist priest, but I realized that in every sick person there is not only a psychological perspective, but also a spiritual one; and that there is a reciprocal relationship, as there is between body and soul, between the physical—the domain of classical medicine—and the propositions of religion."

I was delighted with my colleague's notion of the three dimensions of medicine. But what is this third dimension? My friend Professor Lindeboom, of the Free University of Amsterdam, said to me once that we ought not to talk about the medicine of the person, but of pneumopsychosomatic medicine. The word *psychosomatic* was coined in reference to diseases of the body which derive from a psychological factor. And it is true that for my part I am concerned with the influence of the spiritual life upon disease. Nevertheless I strongly resisted Lindeboom's suggestion, and he readily conceded my point. One cannot talk as if a person were divided into three parts. It is bad enough that we have separated mind and body. It only makes matters worse to try and add a third separate part, the spirit, to the other two, when what we seek is not to compartmentalize, but to reinstate the sense of the person as a whole. Medicine has become specialized, and it would be unrealistic to attempt to study all the specialities in the hope of being able to add them all together. In any case you would still not get the whole. You might be a cardiologist, a rheumatologist, and a psychologist, and still not grasp the whole. It is this sense of the whole that medicine has lost. That is the price we have paid for our great progress in analytical, technical medicine. Even psychosomatic medicine is a purely scientific, objective discipline. Its practitioner is a scientist who studies the relationships between the mind and the body. His function is still to analyze and separate.

If we are to discover the whole, we have to enter into a personal relationship with it. The third dimension, the spiritual dimension, is the dimension of relationship. What is spiritual in a person is the need for relationship—with one's neighbor, with nature, with society, with God. That is the widest definition of the spiritual life. It is what makes man or woman a person, not a body or a psyche, or this or that, but a person. Professor Siebeck of Heidelberg has said that "it is the calling that creates the person." It is because people are called by God that they feel themselves to be persons before God. It is through my personal relationship with my neighbor that I present myself as a person and not as a dispenser of remedies. I have tried to introduce a personal relationship into the doctor-patient situation. It is possible to discuss a wide variety of subjects objectively—science, politics, economics; no personal commitment is involved. Personal commitment takes place only when we talk about our personal lives, each with reference to the other.

The devout Jewish philosopher Martin Buber has said that there are two possible relationships. There is the I–it relationship, which is the objective relationship, the I being the observer who observes the object. That is the position of scientific medicine, which studies human beings as objects, making them things, and preventing the apprehension of the person in the patient. It sees only things in him—his anatomy, his physiology, his psychology, even perhaps his spiritual life, viewed as philosophy. The other possible relationship is I–Thou. No longer is this the relationship of observer and object, but the personal relationship of one subject with another. In order to attain to it the doctor must break away from his or her scientific stance.

We are forced by our civilization to live in a world of things. A pastor from Zaire, the Rev. Masamba ma Mpolo, who is Director of the family ministry section of the WCC, was kind enough to dedicate to me his book, in which appears this noteworthy remark: "Western medicine treats things, whereas African medicine treats persons." You see, he addresses himself to precisely the same questions as I do, and he feels that the doctor has to undergo a process of evolution so as to be able to enter into personal relationship. The whole basis of our civilization is technological, and it accustoms us to looking at everything objectively. So I am very much afraid that in the developing countries what is happening is a dialog of the deaf between the representatives of the West, who are interested in things—all the phenomena studied by medicine—and the people of those countries, who are interested in persons. We of the West try to assert the objectivity of causal relationships; they see mystical relationships between persons. In Western medicine we treat the sick by separating them from their families, taking them to a hospital, attaching them to various machines, in a world of things. In the developing countries medicine treats the patient within his tribe, and, as I have read in Masamba's book, it seeks to resolve the problems of his relationships with his family. As you see, we have here two totally different attitudes: the mechanistic position, which sees only the things that are at hand, and the spiritual vision, which sees the relationship between persons. And it is not easy to make the leap from an objective to a subjective attitude.

For more than thirty years now I have been taking part in meetings of doctors who are seeking ways of tackling that problem. They are known the world over as the Bossey Group, for through my friendship with Pastor Visser't Hooft, the first Secretary-General of the World Council of Churches, we held our first meeting at the Ecumenical Institute at Bossey, near Geneva. The Bossey Group devotes itself to study and research into the medicine of the whole person.

Doctors are great debaters. They could argue very learnedly about the human person for years, studying the anatomy of the brain and the psychological systems of Jung and many others. It is really interesting, but nothing actually happens so far as these doctors are concerned when they argue. If they want to find personal relationship, a change has got to take place in themselves. Argument changes nothing at all. It is no more than an intellectual exercise, and the intellect is only another part of the world of things. These doctors need a personal experience. So I say to each of them, "We shall talk about our work during the day, but in the evening you are going to talk to me about your own life. What made you become a doctor? When have you been ill yourself? What are your own problems, your conflicts with your wife or your children?" Thus, those who come

to Bossey Group meetings know that they will be called
upon to talk about their personal lives. Many doctors
have not dared to come because they are scared. In those
sessions one can see how prone doctors are to hide behind an attitude of objectivity which allows them to give
a fine scientific performance while leaving their personal
problems in the shadows. I have known very famous
doctors who could deliver lecture after lecture with ease,
but whom I found in their rooms sitting in front of a
blank sheet of paper, and saying, "I just don't know
what to say!"

All our education, from infant school onwards, is
aimed at teaching us to be objective. And we all have
great difficulty—and a great fear as well—in being subjective and personal. I myself most of all. I am very shy,
and perhaps because of that I know how serious it is.
But the third dimension intervenes when we give ourselves to another person.

I no longer lead the Bossey Group. That task has been
taken on by younger colleagues who are even bolder
than I was. The last time—in Austria—they said, "We
shall have no more academic discussions. In order to
come really close to each other we shall talk personally
not just in the evening, but throughout the day." It took
some courage, but it worked magnificently! Afterwards
they said they had never experienced anything like it
before: no lectures, no debates, nothing. Just Bible study
and sharing, mutual openness. In the Bossey Group we
have tried to concentrate on the problem of the personal
relationship between doctor and patient, and on all the
other problems of relationships—with one's neighbor,
with nature, with God. That leads on to the problem of
the meaning of things—the meaning of life, of death, of
sickness and health, of healing, of personal life—to
which science has no answer. The only explanation that

science gives is chance. Jacques Monod, Nobel prize-winner for medicine, has said that for science there is only chance and necessity, the necessity of the laws of nature and the chance of the variations which produce something new from time to time.[1] Chance is the god of the scientists. For that reason Lecomte du Noüy, who has worked in the United States for many years, called God "anti-chance." The relationship with God gives a meaning to everything. If there is no God, nothing has meaning. In the scientific perspective the world is seen as a turning wheel, a collection of mechanical phenomena which revolve indefinitely in a random trajectory.

The problem of meaning is a constant preoccupation of mankind. Not infrequently a patient will say to us, "Whatever can I have done to God to deserve an illness like this?" He believes neither in God nor in the devil, but the first thing he thinks of when he falls ill is that it is a punishment sent by God. Everyone asks themselves questions about the meaning of things. Has this sickness that has befallen me got a meaning? And the fact is that the scientific and objective view dismisses meaning. It asserts that the disease has struck by chance, whereas man has an intuitive feeling that there is more in it than chance, and that he has some responsibility for himself. It is this sense of responsibility which gives meaning to life. There is one leading psychologist now who insists on this: Viktor Frankl, who occupies the professorial chair in Vienna once occupied by Sigmund Freud. He has said that in his illustrious predecessor's day the malady of the time was sexual repression. The world has changed since then, and sexuality has been very much brought out into the open. But something else has been repressed, says Frankl: the sense of the meaning of things. We pretend not to care about the meaning of life, when in fact that very question is in everyone's mind.

Albert Camus was preoccupied with this problem of meaning. He tackled it in his first book, *The Myth of Sisyphus*.[2] Is life a labor of Sisyphus, an endless, huge, but fruitless effort by the whole of nature and of mankind? Only religious belief can provide the vision of a goal, a meaning for life, and a meaning for everything in life, including disease, infirmity, and death.

In the Bossey Group we have a German medical scientist, Professor Jores. When he was appointed Rector of Hamburg University, some years ago now, he devoted his inaugural lecture to the subject of the meaning of disease. In the academic atmosphere of the university his words had the effect of a bomb. All of a sudden here was someone setting objectivity aside, and raising a question of conscience. "The more I think about it," he said, "the more certain I am that there is only one possible meaning: the will of God." He alluded to the biblical notion of the fall, in which sickness is seen as a sign that man has fallen out of God's order.

Viktor Frankl says that modern people live in an existential void. Their problem is that they no longer know why they are alive, or whether all their efforts will achieve anything or not. Existentialism is relationship with others, and it is precisely there that the sickness of our time resides. Millions of people, especially in the Western world, no longer know why they are alive. That's something to fall ill about! So, lots of sick people express their despair. Just now I am reading a book by the President of the Association of Psychoanalysts of Switzerland, who lives near me. It is about the meaning of despair. We live in a despairing world, and the problem of despair is related to that of meaning. Frankl has said, "We no longer find sex embarrassing—now it is religion that embarrasses us."

The third dimension of medicine consists, therefore, in helping our patients to become persons, to become aware of their responsibilities. In purely technical medicine they leave the responsibility for their lives in the hands of the doctor. In a three-dimensional medicine they become responsible for themselves once more, because everything takes on meaning the moment we begin to ask ourselves what God is saying to us through sickness.

(That may be compared with what André Frossard tells us in his book *Be Not Afraid!* [Bodley Head, London, 1984] about the conversations which took place between Pope John Paul II and his doctors following the attempt on his life. He quotes Professor Crucitti, the surgeon who operated on the Pope: "He sought to convince us that in the patient-doctor relationship the latter must not be the oracle which sends down its decisions from on high. These decisions ought to be arrived at through a common accord, since though there is on the one hand the skill and knowledge of the medical profession, there is on the other the person's insight and knowledge of himself." André Frossard received from the Pope himself the confirmation that he had tried to help his doctors, explaining to them that the patient, under threat of losing his subjectivity, must fight constantly to regain it and become once more "the subject of his disease" rather than "the object of treatment." This problem of the "depersonalization" of the individual is to be found in all sorts of social relationships, and is, according to John Paul II, one of the gravest problems of the modern world.)

You said that in Africa it is the whole person that is treated, and that the patient is not looked upon as an object. But there is in Africa a strong sense of the community, which we lack. How can we introduce this third dimension of medicine into Western industrialized society?

The Western way of life is the fruit of a unilateral civilization, one that is purely objective and technological. What is wrong with this civilization is the absence of personal relationship. But we shall be unable to restore this sense of personal relationship to society at large unless we already have it in our own lives, within our families and with our patients. The great need of our society is to recover a sense of community. Everywhere we may observe the appearance of small communities which are not great administrative organizations like the churches, but small groups of people in personal relationship with each other. This is the basis of the charismatic movement—small communities, rather fragile perhaps, but demonstrating the need, particularly among the young, to rediscover a form of society which has that sense of community which is lacking in our technological society.

In the past most people had what today seems a luxury: the opportunity to die at home, surrounded by the members of their family. Today, when the decisive moment of death approaches they are whisked off to a hospital. What is your opinion on this?

Formerly one was born and one died in the bosom of one's family. Now we are born amidst a world of things, and we die amidst a world of things. I think that is very sad. It is a sign that human relationships are not looked upon as important. I lost my wife four years ago. We were in Athens, where I was to lecture to an American group. She suffered a coronary thrombosis, and spent a month in a hospital, in intensive care. She received the necessary technological treatment: intensive care is not possible in the home. She spent the necessary period in the hospital, and then happily was well enough to leave, and to join me in our hotel, where we spent the last three days of her life in each other's company, talking a little, being silent a lot, and praying together. It so happened that we talked about her death ten minutes before she died.

I was glad she had left the hospital, even though I visited her there each day. She died at my side, knowing that she was dying, having expressed her fear of death and also her hope of resurrection.

(Long silence.)
There, you see! No one dares to ask any more questions because I spoke of rather personal things. You are well aware of a feeling of malaise as soon as the conversation becomes personal. It upsets the smooth conduct of ideas. We have got to reintroduce personal relationships into our impersonal civilization, and into our hospitals, and into our consulting rooms, and also into our sitting rooms and kitchens.

The only thing that is inevitable in life is death; and yet many of us find it a very difficult subject to talk about.

I am convinced that it is quite natural for people to feel distressed and anxious at the thought of death. In the developing countries death is omnipresent, in a way it is not with us. The dead are as much members of the tribe as the living. All kinds of ceremonies and celebrations bind the tribe to its ancestors. Psychologically it is a much healthier situation than ours, accepting death as something natural. Our civilization is very proud of its technological achievements, but they do not include the abolition of death. So our civilization hides death away. The doctor says that his wish is to comfort the patient. Balint asks who it is that we are comforting, the patient or the doctor? The fact is that we overdo the comfort in order to relieve our own anxiety.

In our proud civilization death is like a slap in the face, for our civilization wants to ignore the divinely ordained limitations on human life. Where will we not go, with our technological progress, with our moon landings and our genetic engineering? Do you not think that we are dreaming of omnipotence, challenging God? We are taking part in that challenge, and our medicine is part and parcel of that proud, scientific civilization. Hence the immense unease when doctors find themselves helpless in the face of death.

Are not the churches of the Protestant tradition making a mistake in suppressing the custom of the funeral vigil? For my part, I think that psychologically and emotionally it may play a very beneficial role. I took part in a vigil in southern Spain. Neighbors and cousins were present. Members of the family could weep together, side by side with their dear ones, and see the body there with them all night long. On the other hand, I discovered that one of my good friends in Geneva, a lady of fifty-nine, had never seen anyone die. She begged me to go and close her husband's eyes if he died. I shall willingly perform that service for her, but I do find it rather extraordinary.

Have you read Dr. Raymond Moody's book *Life after Life?* He questioned people who had been clinically dead but had been brought back to life by modern techniques of resuscitation. Of course they were not yet in the next world, because they came back. But they had nevertheless taken the first steps towards the beyond. As regards the first few minutes after death, all the evidence agreed: people who had been judged by the doctor to be dead, said that they felt as if they were floating near the ceiling, able to survey the scene with the doctor and the nurses leaning over their own body. They heard the doctor say, "He's dead." There is therefore evidence of the persistence of consciousness after clinical death, and before the door to the beyond has opened.

I had not yet read Moody's book when my wife died, but I realized afterwards that she must have been there during my first actions after her death, when I telephoned a colleague to tell him that she had died. According to Moody's evidence she must have heard. There is therefore a period of transition between this life and the beyond. We cannot follow the dead any further, but there is a certain interval between the two. I think that the intermediate stage of the deathwatch was something sacred. I hope that I, at any rate, will not die in a hospital. I hope that I shall be with my family, and that I will know that they will know that I know what I know: a conscious death.

Bearing in mind what you have said about personal relationships, what are we to think about the material conditions under which we practice medicine? Must we bring about changes in our hospitals and our doctors' surgeries in order to facilitate these relationships?

I think that the two aspects are connected. To begin with, doctors themselves have to undergo a change. They must understand the importance of this development, and adapt themselves so as to be ready for a personal relationship when it begins to appear. Doctors who have experienced this sort of relationship no longer work in the same way as before. The spirit is contagious—but there are bound to be repercussions also in the material environment.

I remember one doctor who resigned from a large hospital to serve once again in a small practice where people worked more closely together. I realize, of course, that an act of that sort belongs in the realm of private and personal vocation, and I have no illusions about the difficulty of reintroducing personal relationships into our modern Western hospital service. We need doctors who have come to realize that medicine is a much more profound personal experience if it is practiced in its totality.

I find it hard to accept the idea that disease has a God-given meaning. The New Testament is full of accounts of healing, and I have difficulty in understanding disease which, so far from having meaning, often seems an absurdity.

Your use of the word *absurdity* raises a problem connected with meaning. In their search for a meaning, people are only too ready to imagine God as a severe taskmaster handing out vicious punishments. The day before yesterday I was interviewed by French TV at my home in Troinex, and I spoke about the meaning of disease. Not wishing to give credence to the idea that God sends disease as a punishment, I pointed out that if that were true I should be fighting against God in trying to heal the sick. I asserted that God is always on the side of healing, and that we fight alongside him for healing. But those who are most readily healed are the ones who see a meaning in their sickness. Where sickness has no meaning it inflicts additional suffering.

Do your views imply a need to make changes in the formal training which doctors receive, or are you saying that the attitude you advocate can be acquired only through experience?

I do not think that this specifically personal perspective can be formally taught. On several occasions I have been offered university professorships, either in America or in Europe, and I have always refused, because the capacity for personal relationship is not susceptible of being taught. It can only be communicated from person to person. At any rate, if there are any who can teach it, they do not include me. Today psychology is beginning to figure in the curriculum of medical schools—and not before time! But the medicine of the person cannot be taught. On the other hand, a professor of medicine may well be sensitive to the human perspective of his subject. In my own case, I had a teacher who had this sensitivity to a profound degree, and he communicated it to us at the patient's bedside. As you see, he was not teaching it: he was communicating it.

Do you think that a Christian working in a secular hospital can communicate this attitude without talking about God?

That is up to the individual. Each must ask what it is that God is expecting of him or her, and it is not for me to presume to tell them. We must ask God to show us when we must speak and when we must remain silent. It often happens that we speak when we ought to remain silent, or we remain silent when we ought to speak. The difficulty comes when we feel ourselves obliged to speak.

How do you see the parish contributing to this type of personalized approach, not only in the perspective of the whole person but also in that of the community of the church and of the community in general?

I do not wish to generalize, because the answer must vary from church to church. I have been a member of several different parishes, and I was happiest in a parish in which those in charge were united by close personal ties. It was not just the unity of people who chanced to be working together on a committee—there existed a real personal relationship among them. I believe that this close personal bond between ministers and the church council of a parish has an important bearing on the atmosphere in the church; unfortunately it is within the church that people most tend to hide behind a facade.

I have treated enough church people to know how often in such circles one comes across inhibitions, pharisaism, and aggressiveness, because people are willing to put on a smiling front while harboring all sorts of criticisms in secret. People have told me how they have burst into tears as they came away from a meeting of their church council, because conflicts were being hushed up in order to preserve an appearance of general amity. If this aggressiveness is not allowed to come out into the open—as happens in the rest of society—it can give rise to an anxiety state. I know that I myself am too apt to be afraid of conflict: I try to patch everything up, and only succeed in making matters worse. I realize that Jesus experienced bouts of holy anger. A few days ago my son said to me, "I have never been able to stand up to you, because you never get angry." Actually, I have always been proud of the fact that I never lose my temper, but I see now that it is a disadvantage.

Six

HEALING SOCIETY

Lecture entitled "The Mission of Women in the World"

One day as I was taking part in a conference at Taloires, on the Lake of Annecy, Mme Mac Jannet introduced me to an American who happened to be passing through, telling him, "This is Dr. Tournier. He's writing a book about the mission of women in the world."[1] He looked me straight in the eye, and said with great emphasis, "You've got a nerve!" It is true that I hesitated a little before undertaking the work, particularly as there are some women who are irritated at the thought of a man claiming to talk about their mission. They want to discover it for themselves—which pleases me very much.

In my view it is not so much about women as about our modern world. It is obvious to everybody—sociologists, psychologists, politicians—that Western civilization is sick. There is a tremendous contrast between the technological progress which has made it possible to go to the moon, and even beyond, and the poverty of our individual personal relationships. I think it was in the magazine *Match* that I read an excellent article written by a sociologist who had been doing some research in Africa. You know how they welcome you in

Africa—they take you into their hut, treat you as a member of the family, really spoil you. Our sociologist returns to Paris. At the Charles de Gaulle airport he catches the bus and sees all the passengers sitting side by side. Not a word is exchanged—not even a glance, unless it be one of silent criticism. Some bury themselves in a detective paperback to pass the time. He reflects, "It is we who are the underdeveloped ones!"

It is true that as far as machines go we are overdeveloped, but as regards our qualities as human beings we are underdeveloped. Everyone knows this to be so. Now, who are the ones who are interested in machines? Men. And who are interested in the quality of life? Women. Our civilization has suffered a shift towards its masculine pole. It is ordered in accordance with all the masculine values—possession, power, aggressiveness, scientific objectivity—while the subjective values, that is to say those that concern the heart and our relationships with others, are fearfully deficient. The irrational values, which include religious faith and all the mysteries of human nature, are lost in this desert of machines. You can see it already in young children. A little boy is not given a doll; he is given a model car, and the first thing he does is to take it apart to see how it works. What interests men is seeing how things work. Look at the technical magazines: they are always explaining how things work. And to understand how things work you split them and take them to pieces. At CERN (The European Center for Nuclear Research), in Geneva, the nuclear scientists divide the smallest particles into even smaller pieces to see what they contain. Men go on splitting and dividing without realizing that when all that is left is separate little pieces, they have destroyed the community of the whole. It is women who have a sense of community, women who make the family, make society, make human relationships.

C. G. Jung has explained that both man and woman have technical as well as affective capacities. Man carries within him what Jung called the anima, that is to say the feminine tendency in the human psyche, but he represses his affective capacities and develops his mechanical capacities. Woman, on the other hand, readily suppresses her rational, objective capacities, and gives free reign to her affectivity. But deep within her she has an animus, which gives her masculine capacities. Today's emancipated woman is proving that she is capable of doing everything a man does and which he thought he alone was capable of doing.

During these last few decades we have witnessed the liberation of the *animus* in women, but men for their part have not liberated their *anima*. They are left emotionally handicapped, with great objective, scientific, rational capacities, but at a loss when it comes to giving expression to feelings, to becoming personal. Woman, developed and liberated as she is, has become man's equal, and can play a man's role, whereas man cannot act the woman's part. Or rather, he does not know how to, because he is afraid of emotion. From earliest childhood he has been put on his guard against it. If he fell and hurt himself he was told, "Don't cry! Boys don't cry, only girls cry." Girls have a right to express their feelings, but not boys. Boys have to control themselves, and remain objective. That is what mothers teach their sons—in fact the whole educational process tends to make a man suppress his feelings, whereas a woman is permitted to express them.

Not long ago I went to Munich to talk to some Americans. A well-known American writer, whom I had met before, introduced me in the customary manner: "Dr.

Tournier needs no introduction from me," he said, "you all know who he is and the insight he has brought us with his concept of the person." I burst out laughing. He was rather taken aback, and asked, "Is that not right?" I replied, "It is not the concept of the person that I am interested in—it is the person itself!" Men are only too ready to talk about concepts. My whole aim is to convey a message about the person, and yet I was being introduced as if the important thing about me was that I had a concept. A person, unlike a concept, has two eyes, a mouth. . . . We have to get back to a sense of the human, and free ourselves of the abstractions of ideas and concepts. In order to do so we must overcome man's resistance against removing his mask, uncovering himself, showing himself as he is, presenting himself as a person.

Men are not very talkative at home, a point which has always been remarked upon by psychologists. Women talk much more than men. Women have said to me, "To get to know my husband a bit better, I invite our friends to the house, because he then tells them things that I know absolutely nothing about." The husband does not realize that he is secretive towards his wife. I remember one worthy man who came to my consulting room and told me straight out that he had not come to see me about a marriage problem, as so many people probably did, because he was lucky enough not to have any such troubles . . . .

"Good for you!" I said. "You are an exception."

"You see, we promised each other from the start that we would always be completely open with each other, and we've kept our word. No secrets—we tell each other everything."

"Ah! I congratulate you."

We talked for an hour. He told me about very serious problems he was having in his professional life, as well as in his spiritual life. Then, as I was seeing him off, I said to him:

"Tell me, what does your wife say about all this?"

"My wife? She knows nothing about it. I don't talk to her about things like that."

He was being sincere, perfectly sincere, when he declared, "We tell each other everything." What he did not realize was that he no longer talked to her about the really personal things.

The one thing that releases the floodgates in a man is sexual desire. When he is in love he talks, and the girl is struck all of a heap by this young man as he tells her all sorts of exciting stories about the pranks he got up to at school, the pals he had—he could hardly be more personal. Everything is wonderful, and they will get on together magnificently! Then they are married, and as soon as the man has got what he wants, namely the satisfaction of possessing a woman, he says nothing any more, or at least it is no longer like it was before. The sad thing is that sometimes he does find his tongue again, but now it is with the pretty secretary to whom he has taken a fancy. He feels that she understands him better than his wife does, and he begins to tell her all the personal things which he hides from his wife. You can see how dangerous it is, because it is only through sexual desire that our man recovers the ability to talk the language of the emotions. It is vital, therefore, for married couples to maintain their dialog. Man has a sense of the objective, while woman has a sense of the subjective. Our world is constructed in the image of man, highly developed as regards material things and the machines that fascinate men, but very poor as regards the commitment of people to each other.

Who is it who has a sense of the person? It is woman; and I recall a little incident in my own married life which showed me that this was so. I am indebted to my wife for everything that I have to say about women, because I was even more uncommunicative than most. We were discussing the subject of divorce, and I was expounding some grand theory when my wife interrupted me:

"But who is it you're talking about?"

"I'm not talking about anyone. I'm talking about the problem of divorce."

I realized then that what interests a woman is not the problem of divorce, but Margaret's or Sheila's or Joan's divorce. It was a revelation for me. I said to myself, "Here am I—I've been preaching about the person all over the place for thirty or forty years, and I still don't have a sense of the person." The world, of course, also exists, and it is my task as a man to study the problems of society. But, in common with all men, I do not have a sense of the person.

Man always has in him something of the schoolmaster who teaches and explains, who has concepts which leave a woman lost in amazement: "My! Isn't that interesting! Isn't that marvelous!" But it never enters his head that he might be missing something that he could learn. The philosopher Martin Buber, who spent many years in Zurich,[2] showed that there are two kinds of relationships between the human person and the world around him. One is an objective relationship, in which the observer is neutral and impersonal. The observer is not engaged, and sees without being seen. That is the scientific attitude. The other is a relationship in which the individual does make a commitment. Buber took the example of a tree. One might consider a tree scientifically, botanically, chemically, as a mere object, a thing; but one can talk to it. To talk to a tree is to rediscover a bond with nature. I remember a medical conference in which a woman psychoanalyst from Zurich told us the story of her painful, lonely childhood. There was a certain tree to which she used to go each evening to tell it about her little troubles. And the tree would reply, "I understand." No one understands us better than nature.

There are two possible relationships. They are not in conflict, since they are complementary: except that in our modern civilization the objective relationship has been enlarged. From our cradles onwards we are taught about things, not about persons. We learn to see the world as a big machine turning, turning with its stars, its electrons, and even its chickens making eggs and its eggs making chickens; a meaningless roundabout, always turning but going nowhere. We are presented with this scientific view of the world from our infant classes right up to our doctorates in philosophy. Philosophers tell us in vain that we ought to be personal—they themselves do not manage to be so, for they too do not progress beyond concepts.

My daughter-in-law is an artist, and I like her pictures very much. She is a member of the Society of Women Painters. Why did women painters form such a society? In order to protect themselves against the imperialism of men, because everyone considers that a picture painted by a woman is less serious than one by a man—a book by a female author less serious than one by a male author, a woman's philosophy less serious than a man's. So there is a Society of Women Painters, and my daughter-in-law said to me:

"We are organizing an exhibition at the Rath Museum on such and such a date, and one of my canvases has been selected. It's a self-portrait."

"Oh! I must go and see that. It's some time away yet. I'll ask you about it nearer the day."

Time passed, and one day I asked my daughter-in-law: "Now, that exhibition, when is it?"

"But it's already happened!" And then she sweetly added, "If it had been your son exhibiting a picture instead of me, I bet you wouldn't have forgotten."

The shaft went home. I do not think that she was alluding to the ties of blood between me and my son. My daughter-in-law knows, in common with all women, that she carries less weight than a man. If a man gives us a letter to post, we do not forget, but if it is the wife. . . .

Women count for rather less. What does that mean? It means they are despised. The word is a strong one. Perhaps the right thing to say would be that women are looked down on, but I prefer to say that they are despised. Even I, keen as I am on the need for men to liberate their repressed feelings, had forgotten my daughter-in-law's exhibition. Many men openly hold women in contempt, which allows a man to let a woman talk to him all evening without uttering a single word in reply, whereas if he had been with one of his men friends, he would have been responding to every remark.

A fortnight ago I was attending one of a series of learned international conferences which are held biennially in Geneva, to which there come large numbers of philosophers and others from a wide range of academic disciplines. The theme was "The Demand for Equality." People want equality, they vote for equality, but equality does not happen. So for a whole week we discussed with those erudite philosophers the subject of equality, only to conclude that it is unattainable. A professor from the Sorbonne came to explain to us that the motto of France, "Liberty, Equality . . ." is impracticable because if there is liberty there is no equality, and if there is equality there is no liberty. It was a question of yes, but. We ought to have equality, but if we did have it, it would be a disaster, because if we were all equal it would be unbearably monotonous. I said to myself—I said it out loud, in fact—that the true problem is contempt. "Don't despise me. Take me seriously." That is what lies behind every claim for equality. Take me seriously, even if I haven't a university degree, even if I am only a laborer, even if I am black, even if I am an immigrant, even if I am a woman, even if I am an old age pensioner, even if I am only a little child. The claim is not so much for equality as for dignity, to be taken seriously, to be recognized as a person with something valid to say, not merely in an argument, but in a dialog.

Like everybody else, I thought that this contempt on the part of men had always existed, and that, for example, the status of women was worse in the Middle Ages than it is now. "In our present struggle," the feminists say, "we must fight against the medieval status imposed on women." Actually it is far from the truth that women were more victimized in the Middle Ages than they are nowadays. In my book *The Gift of Feeling*, on the mission of women in the world, I relied on the work of a French historian, Régine Pernoud, who demonstrates that the status of women in the Middle Ages was much higher than it was when I was a boy.

In the Middle Ages men and women were equal before the law. They voted—rarely, it is true, and only in local elections—but women voted as well as men. There was even one woman whose claim to fame was that she voted no when all the rest of her commune voted yes. Women were as cultured as men. The small educated minority of the population was to be found in the convents and monasteries. The women's convents outnumbered the monasteries, and the nuns were as cultured as the

monks. They knew Greek and Hebrew; there were
women poets, writers, and politicians. Eleanor of Aqui-
taine, who became Queen of England, exercised more
political power than any one person today. Equality was
a fact of life. There was even one convent, that of Fon-
tevrault, which had both men's and women's sections,
under the authority not of a man but an abbess, who
had been promoted to that office at the age of twenty-
five. These religious houses became the centers of a sort
of political general post—kings and queens retired to
them, and others of their inmates came out to mount
royal thrones. They built a civilization based on a specific
scale of values. Nowadays our values are power, science,
material gain. In the nineteenth century people still
imagined that the great epic of scientific discovery was
at last about to bring peace and universal knowledge.
In the twentieth we have certainly got over that! It has
led us instead to the atomic bomb.

Civilization has lost its way. In losing God it has lost
the very meaning of life. It is necessary to recover a
human scale of values, within the church as well as outside it, since the church is often even more backward
than the world outside. Theology has become abstract.
In order to become a minister of the church it is not
necessary to have the gift of relating to others. What is
required is a degree—that is to say the ability to do scientific work, such as biblical exegesis. Personal relationships are to be found in the small communities, but not
in the big churches. One Easter Day I was in my own
church of St. Gervais, in Geneva. After the sermon there
is always a moment's pause to allow those who do not
wish to stay for the celebration of the Lord's Supper to
depart. The thought came to me, "On my right is my
wife, whom I do know a little, and on my left is someone
I do not know at all. I could take the opportunity of

introducing myself." If you only knew! My heart was thumping in my breast. Did I dare speak? I went through a sort of crisis, with the sweat pouring from me, before I was able to lean over and say, "I am Dr. Tournier." He was a peasant from the Canton of Vaud. After the celebration, outside the church, he came up to me, shook me by the hand, and said, "It's nice, this custom you have in Geneva of introducing yourselves to each other."

Another book I relied upon was one by Francoise Dolto, who is widely known through her talks on French radio. I never met her myself, though I knew her husband, who was also a doctor—he once gave me a box of a dozen ties as a hint that I ought to dress more smartly. Francoise Dolto wrote a fine book on the gospel as through the eyes of a psychoanalyst. Her understanding of Jesus is different from ours because she is a woman, and as I read her book I regretted that theology has been an almost exclusively masculine study. She shows that Jesus listened to women, not just like the husband who says, "Go on talking, it will do you good," but because he expected to hear something. At the wedding in Cana it was his mother whom he asked about whether it was time to begin his ministry. And in the end it was Mary of Bethany who signified to him that the moment had come for him to go up to Jerusalem and to the cross.

Our civilization is sick because the feminine values have been suppressed, and men suffer for it even if they do not realize the fact. So whenever possible I say to women: Be women. Do not go about trying to act like men. Offer the world what men are incapable of offering.

Seven

THE ENIGMA OF SUFFERING

A lecture delivered in Montreux

I at once accepted the invitation to come and speak to you here in Montreux, because I was told that I should be addressing a united meeting of both Protestant and Catholic parishes, and that pleases me very much indeed. It is important for Christians to meet to tackle problems together, and if there is one subject that lends itself to this kind of collaboration it is the problem of suffering, which is the same for Protestants, for Catholics, and for everyone else.

A few months ago we took a similar step in my little Genevan village of Troinex, in the countryside near the French border. Except that in Troinex there are three churches: Protestant, Catholic, and Armenian Orthodox. We organized a Christian gathering of all three congregations, and the speaker was Suzanne Fouché, a well-known French Catholic. Suzanne Fouché has more right than I have to talk about suffering, since she has suffered far more than I have. I have observed suffering, and I have also personally suffered a little, but it is those who have suffered the most who ought to speak.

Suzanne Fouché wrote a book entitled *Souffrance, école de vie* (*Suffering, a School of Life*) in which she tells the story of her life. She had intended to become a doctor, but at the age of sixteen or seventeen she contracted tuberculosis of the spinal column. She spent twenty years on her back in bed, her studies interrupted, immobilized and alone. Imagine that broken life! However, though broken, her life was far from sterile. It was extremely fertile. In the sanatorium at Berck-sur-Mer, Suzanne Fouché saw the harmful effects on the inmates of their enforced idleness. She conceived the idea of inviting them to adopt a more active attitude. She gave them this admonition: "Do what you can!" That was the start of the Suzanne Fouché League, which has now grown to the point where she heads an organization of more than thirty houses all over France, where infirm and physically handicapped people are rehabilitated. Her principle is that people who have been struck down by disability must be retrained for a job which means a step up the social ladder. In this way they will have access to a better life as a compensation for the inferiority created by their disability.

I had asked her to talk to us, at Troinex, about the connection between her charitable work and her inner life, between her work and her dedication of her life to Jesus Christ. In the course of a tremendous crisis of revolt against her fate, against the fact that her life and her intended career had been brought to a halt, she underwent the experience of acceptance, and her career was, in a way, given back to her. She even became much more than a doctor. Only the other day I was up near Paris, addressing more than a score of doctors who work under her direction. There are many more all over France.

I first met Suzanne Fouché a good many years ago in a conference of Catholic doctors organized by Professor Delord, of Lyon, in the Jesuit house of Annecy. I had been told that Suzanne Fouché would be there, and so I looked out for her. When we met I told her how I had been looking forward to meeting her. She replied that she had been told that Paul Tournier would be there. "And so I came to hear you speak." We both had a good laugh, and ever since then we have been close friends. She has taken part in the doctors' conferences that I have been organizing for the past twenty-five years. I wish to take this opportunity to say a few words about them.

Shortly after the end of the war my wife and I had occasion to go to Germany. Apart from the troops we were almost the first foreigners to enter the country. There was devastation everywhere. Picture the situation in 1946: it was known that doctors, under the diabolical rule of the Nazis, had been turned into agents of death instead of being agents of life. We met some of the foremost German scientists, who were reflecting on what had happened and who realized that medicine, in becoming a purely technical affair, had lost is profound inspiration. It had been rendered powerless in the face of the power of the state, and the latter had been able to induce doctors to perform acts which conscience condemns. What had happened in the case of medicine was true also of other disciplines, such as law. They had fallen under the power of the state because they no longer had any solid spiritual base.

In its origin medicine was almost a priestly mystery, closely bound to religion. Now, with the development of modern science, it has become neutral. Doctors have come to the point of saying, "Good heavens, the question of religion has nothing to do with us. We do our duty—there is no ethic other than scientific integrity." Looking back on the tragedy of Nazism, one realized the extreme danger inherent in that kind of neutrality, in the way it put medicine at the mercy of political or social pressures.

The idea of the German Lutheran Church in organizing these meetings was that in order to reconstruct a sound outlook it was necessary to take people profession by profession and help them to rethink their profession in the light of the gospel. From this grew the idea of organizing similar gatherings on an international level, open to all the various specialties and to all denominations. In 1947, before Vatican II, and even before the foundation of the World Council of Churches at Amsterdam, before the Orthodox Churches had joined in the ecumenical movement, this was something quite new.

The aim was to rediscover the very sources of medicine. Medicine concerns itself with man. Science, for its part, sees only man's component parts; it is essentially analytical—that is to say, it divides and subdivides down to the tiniest detail. The more it subdivides, the more clearly it sees. It can tell you what the liver is, what the kidneys are; it can analyze the sixteen functions of the liver and detect thirty-two kinds of rheumatism. But the whole is missing. Science can never apprehend it. Open any textbook: you will find descriptions of the symptoms of every disease, but what disease is you will not find. It will describe all man's organs, but what is human it will not say. The things that pertain to wholeness are beyond the purview of science. If we are to arrive at an understanding of the nature of human beings, of disease, of life, of healing, we must complement our scientific knowledge, which is technical and analytical, with perspectives of a different, non-scientific order—the spiritual.

Do not misunderstand me! I am not advocating the rejection of science. The greatest scientists are the ones who understand that science has its limitations. They know that two things go to the making of a doctor—

great scientific competence and a great heart. And scientific training cannot produce the great heart! The ability to relate, to enter into contact with one's patient, to be open with him, to become his friend—all this has nothing to do with science, and must come from a different source.

For thirty-five years these sessions have been taking place in various countries, with colleagues from America, Europe, Asia, coming together to seek to define a Christian position in medicine. I do not mean a "Christian medicine," because there is only one medicine. But Christianity can enlighten the doctor by helping him or her to understand what man is, what disease is, and what suffering is.

I am very glad to have collaborated in this way, almost before it happened, with the great ecumenical movement of our times. In fact I have found a welcome in traditions other than the Protestantism to which I belong. My first book, *Médecine de la personne*, was translated into Italian by a young colleague who is now a professor in Rome and president of the organization of Catholic doctors in Italy. It was published by a Catholic publishing house. I wrote a book entitled *Bible et Médecine* which was translated into Spanish by a well-known doctor. He had warned me that a book about the Bible by a Protestant would not be easy to publish in Spain. It would need the Catholic Church's visa, the *nihil obstat*. It took a long time, but I am proud to have the *nihil obstat* on the Spanish edition of my book. What this means is that doctors can create a bond that transcends denominational barriers, and even barriers between different religions. I have had contacts with Islam, and I have been able to gauge the possibility of uniting not only Christians, but also Jews and Moslems, in a spiritual view of man.

Doctors are much given to argument, and in these sessions it is fairly easy to have discussions about the human race, about disease, about the Bible, and about suffering. But if something solid is to be created, the doctor must go beyond discussion and become personal. Therefore in the evening we ask the doctors to talk about their own lives and their own experiences. It is most interesting, for instance, to hear doctors talking one after another about their experiences when they themselves were ill. There is something very impressive in the diversity of suffering and the diversity of people's reactions to it. One can sense how manifold are the resonances of the human heart. It is good for doctors to experience sickness, but their memories are short; and so if they are asked to tell us in our meetings what they felt when they were ill, it makes them human again. You know what doctors are like—they tend to be up in the air. It is all this "Yes, doctor; very good, doctor" treatment they receive. Everybody gives way to them. They have to get down from their pedestals if they are to become human, and being ill themselves does precisely that for them.

You asked me to say something about the Christian attitude to suffering. I think that one can look at the subject in three different ways: the Christian's attitude to his or her own suffering; the Christian's attitude to the suffering of others; and the Christian's attitude to the problem of suffering.

This old stock problem of philosophy, the problem of suffering, together with that of evil, has never ceased to torment humankind, and no sage, no writer, has got very far with it. A historical-philosophical account of the problem of evil would lead us rather far afield. It is clear at any rate that no solution has ever been found. The Greeks had attempted a rational approach to it, and

Jesus appeared at a point when Greek philosophy was rejoicing in a triumphant rationalism in which everything fitted perfectly together. Jesus, for his part, never treated the problem of suffering in abstract terms, as a theory, a doctrine, or a philosophical proposition: he told stories, he met the sick and healed them, he lived and suffered himself. Jesus appears in an abstract world, so intellectually cultured that it has lost contact with reality. His message is essentially concrete. He does not answer problems abstractly, but by acting, intervening. His approach both to the sick and to the healthy is through living experience, through story and parable. He touches us not through our intellect, but in the reality of our problems.

From beginning to end the Bible affirms that suffering and the presence of evil are characteristics of our world. It describes the world as fallen, a world which has lost its original perfection. Thus the Genesis story which sets out the fact of the fall in poetic form, demonstrates the fundamental idea that God created the world perfect, but that there took place a breakdown that brought disease, suffering, and death in its train. All these enemies are signs of the disorganization which the Bible calls the fall. Picking up this idea in his letters to the Romans—almost at the other end of the Bible—St. Paul says, "Through sin death entered the world." Thus a connection was made between disobedience and the state of suffering in which we live. In Genesis God says to the man, "With sweat on your brow shall you eat your bread" and to the woman, "You shall give birth to your children in pain." These texts have been taken to mean that God has inflicted a punishment upon mankind because of its disobedience, and I have known colleagues who have said to me, "Now that we can have childbirth without pain, does that mean that we are acting contrary to God's will?"

That is not quite the point. One of my friends who is both a lawyer and a doctor, Professor Jacques Ellul of Bordeaux, explains that it was not God's intention to lay down a penalty, but rather to point out to man the consequences of his fall: "You wanted to spread your wings and act on your own? Well, you shall see what happens." That is the meaning of the fruit of the knowledge of good and evil: no longer needing God to direct one's life. I share this view completely. In the Genesis texts and in the spirit of the Bible, God warns man that if he tries to do without him and control his own life, he is in for a lot of suffering. It is not so much a sanction as a warning.

In the early part of the biblical revelation the notion of suffering and nonsuffering is bound up with that of the obedience and disobedience of the people of Israel. The language is collective. But with the prophets there enters the notion of the individuality of obedience, of personal responsibility. The question then arose as to whether obeying God ensured good health, and disobeying him brought disease. This is the crisis of conscience that is tackled in the book of Job.

Job is the man who suffers every kind of misfortune without having done anything against God. Not only does he fall ill, but he loses his wife, his children, his cattle, along with everything else. Furthermore, he has friends who, under the pretext of comforting him, drum it into him that if he suffers all these misfortunes it must be because he is a great sinner. But Job protests: it's not true, it's not true! The book of Job is a story, of course, a fiction; but it raises the eternal problem—is suffering a punishment? Such an interpretation is refuted, not only by the author of the book of Job, but also by the prophets Jeremiah and Isaiah.

Then Jesus comes. They bring him a man born blind, and his disciples ask, "Who sinned, the blind man or his parents?" Jesus' reply is categorical: "Neither the blind man, nor his parents." We have here a rigorous, clear, definite, absolute, textual denial on the part of Jesus. I could deal at length with this point, but this one text is sufficient to show that Jesus was marking an important turning point. Suffering is bound up with the fallen state of the human race which he came to save, but at the same time he refused to consider suffering as the consequence either of personal sin or of the collective sin of a community. This marks considerable progress.

The Bible, then, asserts that there is a link between the fall and suffering, which is a sign of the fallen state of humanity, but it assures us at the same time that the sick are no more sinners than those who are well. I say, therefore, to those who are well, "Beware of pharisaism and realize that you are all sinners, along with the sick."

We do often find a certain complacency on the part of those who are well in their attitude to those who are sick, as if their state of health indicated superior moral worth. The sick are not slow to feel it. Jesus brings something quite different—the notion of a God who saves. The idea is already there in the Old Testament, when God contemplates people from on high and sees all their abominations. The text has it that he is provoked— "Such men are smoke in my nostrils, an ever burning fire." This image of God's nose burning red in his anger is a picturesque way of speaking which attributes human feeling to God. His anger flares frequently in the Old Testament. But passion itself means suffering. So here we have the Old Testament bearing witness to the suffering of God at the sins of men. Jesus goes much further, and introduces a truly stupendous notion.

Do you know that Christianity is the only religion of the suffering God? All religions have aimed at portraying God in the most attractive, the sublimest possible light: a God in apotheosis—a God of health, dare I say?—a God of perfection. Christianity is the more astonishing because it presents a God who suffers, who suffers with each sick person, who accompanies each sick person in his or her suffering, who suffers with the suffering of each sick person. This is the great Christian message for the sick: God suffers from your sickness. Those who say "I cannot believe in God when I see all the horrors in the world" fail to understand that the one who sees all the horror most clearly is God himself, and that he suffers from all the evil and all the suffering of humanity. With Jesus, it is not only the God who suffers because of the suffering of others, but the God who suffers himself. Jesus on the cross takes upon himself a suffering which he has not deserved, the supreme denial of the false link between sin and sickness.

The gospel has brought about a complete transformation of the problem of suffering. Despised and looked upon as an unavoidable burden in the ancient world, suffering is all but cancelled out when those who suffer become the well-beloved of God. One only has to think of the martyrs who ran joyfully to meet the lions with hymns on their lips. This transfiguration of suffering is a quite extraordinary historical event. The church has even had to resist a certain tendency to pursue perfection by means of suffering. I note in passing the following exhortation by Pope Pius XII: "Suffering must never be made an end, but it may be a means in the hands of God."

There have been other interpretations which I should like to touch upon. Some have tried to resolve the problem by denying evil, denying the reality of suffering. To assert "I am not suffering" may demonstrate great virtues of faith, and subjective spirits may have some success that way, but it is not a biblical solution. On the contrary, the Bible looks suffering in the face. You might say that the Bible is the book of suffering.

Other Christians stress the power of healing through the Spirit. They too witness to great faith, but through concentrating on the victories of faith, they neglect part of the gospel, particularly the cross. We see a goodly number of patients who have turned to faith healing. It can do good, but it can also do harm: "If people of faith, who believe in the power of the Holy Spirit, have tried to heal me but have failed, that must be because I am unworthy of salvation and God's healing." We are back to the idea of guilt. You can understand why a doctor is sensitive to the danger of interpretations which re-create a sort of shame at being ill. The sick are prone to being ashamed of their sickness, of being a nuisance to their family and friends, of being useless. The doctor is therefore very cautious in the face of any triumphalist attitude which cannot be justified in all circumstances.

The Christian attitude, to conclude this first part on the problem of suffering, is above all an attitude of humility. The humility to recognize that there are no answers to the problems in our minds. Kharim Aga Khan, the leader of a Muslim sect, once said to a journalist who asked him if suffering came from God, "I do not permit myself to ask that question." That is a lesson for us, and entirely within the biblical perspective. God has mysteries. God has secrets which we cannot penetrate. In fact I ought to be silent, but you have asked me to speak. So I speak in order to point out that there is no answer, that the Christian line is not to penetrate the mysteries of God, but to bow before them. "The world is inexplicably mysterious and full of suffering," wrote Albert

Schweitzer. Both a Christian and a doctor, Schweitzer recognized the immensity of human suffering. He devoted himself to its relief, but he recognized the mystery and accepted it.

Christianity has more to say in respect of the second part of my subject, "the Christian's attitude to the suffering of others," because it introduces compassion into human history. Before that, the weak, the helpless, the wounded, were the object of scorn. They were good for nothing but to be rejected. Jesus, both in his life and in his teaching, attaches a quite special importance to them. This caused a complete reversal, and even non-Christian countries live under the historical influence of this modification of the public mind. Henceforth the powerless, the children, the sick are the subject of compassion instead of the turned back and the shrugged shoulder.

The Christian in face of the suffering of others is the man called by God, through the bond of faith, to go to the help of others to relieve their suffering. The parables of the good Samaritan and the good shepherd have tremendous importance for the doctor. In them he hears God's call to go to the assistance of others, and that gives his vocation its true dimension. The doctor becomes a fellow worker with God.

Suffering is immense. We do not know where it comes from, but God is not indifferent to it, and God sends his servants to relieve it. God may even transfigure the suffering and cause those who suffer most to bring forth most fruit. I return to the example of Suzanne Fouché whose ministry to the disabled has been so fruitful because she herself was able to adopt a Christian attitude of acceptance of suffering.

The sentiment of human sympathy has enlarged greatly in our generation. We know how indifferent

Christians could be to distant sufferings. Nowadays, when some catastrophe is made known, there is an immediate reaction on the part of all those who can no longer accept that they can be happy and free from worry so long as there is any suffering on earth. At the same time the Bible is realistic: there will always be the poor, there will always be people suffering. The way of the cross accepts suffering, accepts failure, accepts not being able to achieve definitive victory.

Kierkegaard, one of the greatest Christians among the world's thinkers, said on his deathbed, "My life is a great suffering, unknown by others, and incomprehensible." He underlined the incommunicable character of suffering. We shall never really be able to measure the suffering of others. We can guess at it. The phrases we use, such as "I know how you feel!" are often little more than cant. Those who suffer know very well that their suffering is incommunicable, and that we are failing to appreciate the problem if we think that we can put ourselves in their place. An inconsolable widow came to see me. I said to her, "Upon my word, madame, not having lost my wife I find it very difficult to understand what being widowed means." She was very surprised, and said to me, "All the others have tried to console me. You're the first man who's told me the truth!" That widow became an active and wonderful Christian. So many of the things one says, supposedly to comfort a person, don't comfort anyone because they do not carry the ring of truth. It has to be said that no one can, like Christ, have total compassion. We all have our limitations, and they are particularly evident in the face of death. Doctors, whose keenest wish is to come to the aid of the sick, are quite thrown by the fatally ill. Many doctors have admitted to me that once they could do nothing more, they found it difficult to visit a patient whom they looked upon as already lost.

I read in a book that an American psychologist once installed himself in a hospital corridor in New York. Having checked which rooms contained people who were dying and which contained patients making good progress, he noted with a stopwatch how long it took the nurses to answer a call. He found that they responded twice as quickly to calls from the patients who were recovering, compared with those who were dying. He spoke to them about it, and they were astonished—"No, no!" they said. "We run as soon as the light goes on . . . Anyway, we don't know whether the calls come from a patient who is dying or from one of the others." And yet the observation was not mistaken, so their action was unconscious. Each of us has a certain fear of suffering, and we share the sufferings of others up to a certain limit. This is true even of the most religious among us. The same author quotes cases of pastors who, in order to avoid a more personal exchange, turn to reading verses from the Bible. People can die quite alone in hospitals. They die alone in a kind of conspiracy of silence.

I must now tackle the last theme: "the Christian's attitude to his own suffering." To accept! Acceptance is difficult. Passive reaction and resignation have no virtue. Old people who go to die in a corner are more like injured animals than human beings. Rebellion! That is the usual reaction, and no one need be ashamed of feeling rebellious when fate strikes him. Most people hide it, but the first reaction, the normal reaction in the eyes of a psychologist or a doctor, is revolt. Open your Bible, and you will see that the greatest believers were rebels— Isaiah, Jeremiah, and all the rest. There were even movements of rebellion in Jesus himself. So do not be ashamed of rebellion. It is normal. It is necessary to be able to pass through this zone of indignation in order to reach true acceptance, not by an effort of the will, but with the present help of the Spirit.

The purpose of life is not the absence of suffering, but that the suffering should bear fruit. Jesus warned his followers that they would experience tribulation and persecution. And St. Francis said, "The good that I wait for is so great that all pain is a joy to me." That is the triumph of the Spirit and of faith which can transform suffering into the joy of knowing God more intimately.

When my younger son broke his leg he said, "At last something's happened to me!" We had been trying so hard to protect him from every danger that he had the feeling of not really being alive. If one does not suffer, one does not live. I have seen people discovering that they were alive through the experience of suffering. It can make us cry out to God. Calvin, who suffered from stomach pains, would exclaim, in his vivid way, "Oh, my God, you are grinding me!" How many of the saints have had this experience of the transformation of suffering, not in a philosophical sense, as if it were God who sent it, but in the sense of being turned by it towards God? And what can the meaning of life be, if it is not to find God?

In the book of Job, to which I have referred, there is no answer to the problem of the suffering of the righteous, though God has his thunderings and his lightnings flashing in the clouds—which rather shocked the philosopher Jung, who felt that God was in the wrong in leaving Job without an answer. In the end, however, Job meets God and says, "I knew you only by hearsay; but now I have seen you with my own eyes." Yes, suffering can be the occasion of meeting God. I am reminded of a mother who had lost her daughter who was in the prime of her life. She came to see me and said, "From now on I have a link with heaven." So, a very grievous bereavement can create a solidarity with heaven. We have one foot in heaven because our treasure is already there, and we long to rejoin it.

My last point touches on the problem of meaning. The person who finds no meaning in life suffers doubly. He suffers the suffering itself, and he suffers from the feeling that it is pointless. One of the great leaders of modern psychoanalysis, Viktor Frankl of Vienna, has stressed the human need to find meaning in life. Since the time of Freud certain of his followers have tried to see psychoanalysis as a panacea for all the problems of mankind. Freud, who was an honest man, warned them against this when he said, "Psychoanalysis may very well transform a neurotic suffering into a human suffering, but human suffering goes further—psychoanalysis cannot do anything for it."

Freud himself suffered fearfully. He underwent thirty-two operations for cancer of the larynx, over a period of ten years, and ended up unable to eat, drink, or speak. A man of very great humility and steadfastness, he put up with it all with extraordinary stoicism. We have traveled a long way from Freud, who said, "Human suffering is beyond our scope," to Frankl who says, "Man's greatest need is to find a meaning in things, a meaning in life." Modern people suffer from a void of meaning, which Frankl calls the existential void. Most of our contemporaries are carried away as in a whirlwind by a mass production, consumer-orientated civilization which goes meaninglessly round and round.

You understand what we are struggling for! Our aim is to help humanity to look at things no longer only in their technological, external, inhuman aspect, but also to see what is at stake on the human level, in the life of every person. This is the struggle of faith which can find meaning even in suffering, in failure and amputation, and win through to intimacy with the Savior.

The heart of the gospel is not a doctrine, but a person, a suffering being. In suffering, the Christian can approach Jesus and identify with him, in his death and in his victory. The maturity of the person, the full growth of the spiritual being, do not come about, alas! without suffering, or at least without communion with the suffering of others.

Catholics employ a notion which is unfamiliar to Protestants—the idea of offering up their suffering, and I think it is up to me as a Protestant doctor to say that they are right. St. Paul speaks of his sufferings as a way of making up all that has still to be undergone by Christ. "I live now not with my own life but with the life of Christ who lives with me," he says. This identification with Jesus is a well-known psychological phenomenon. It is called communion. Union with Jesus unites us with others in the certainty that the supreme hope is beyond this world, in a new earth and a new order where, as the book of Revelations says, there will be no more death, and no more mourning or sadness.

One may say that society today accepts it has a responsibility to relieve suffering, but it is still uncertain in its attitude towards death. Ought not medical personnel to be given some training that would put them on their guard against the attitudes which you referred to in the case of the American nurses?

It is needed as much by doctors as by nurses! The silence on the subject of death is a kind of connivance, in which each person tries to reassure himself or herself by talking about something else. We know that people are well aware that they are going to die, that they must die, and yet we are afraid of talking about it to the dying person. We think that we are sparing the person's feelings, but it is our own feelings we are afraid of. Psychologically it is a taboo, a thing that must not be touched. If we were to tackle the taboo perhaps we should succeed in demystifying it, as happened with sex when we began to talk about it freely and straightforwardly. In the Far East there are countries where things are arranged differently: an old man will have his coffin made up and placed in the drawing room so that his family and friends can come and admire it in advance. There is nothing inhuman about this familiarity with death—it may even, in a way, be very beautiful.

This taboo about death darkens our lives enormously. We act as if death did not exist, and that is a kind of lie. Death is the inevitable passage to another stage of life, to be compared with birth. The child in its mother's womb knows nothing of where it is going. It learns only from experience, and we too will learn from our own experience about the world beyond death. Even those who are already persuaded of that, like you and me, have reservations when it comes to being completely straightforward and honest about death. The victory must therefore be won in ourselves first, and then we can do something to help the rest of mankind.

I knew a couple. The man knew that the wife was dying, and she knew it too, but up to the last moment they never spoke to each other about it. Doctors themselves don't agree about the propriety of telling someone he is going to die.

Perhaps I replied rather hastily just now, and you are right. We must use tact. Everything depends on the level of communion, the degree of intimacy, between the people concerned. I have a surgeon friend who was the medical director of a large hospital. His son contracted cancer at the age of seventeen, and died slowly over a whole year. During all that time the lad never stopped expressing confidence in his father: "My dad will cure me." The father often came to Geneva to unburden his heart to me, and he used to say, "I have to steel myself to go in and see the boy—he's going steadily towards death, and yet he tells everyone. 'I have confidence in my dad, he'll cure me.' "

The boy died and the years passed. Eight years later my surgeon friend met one of his son's closest friends, who told him: "Your son knew he was dying. He talked to me about it once, and he said, 'I need to keep my dad happy, so I tell everyone he'll make me well again.' "

You see the drama: the father knowing the son was dying, the son knowing he was dying but repeating, "I have confidence in my dad, he'll cure me," in order to avoid the emotion and to please his father; and this "I have confidence" which breaks his father's heart and sets up a wall between them. They were never able to talk together. The father was distraught by the suffering and the bereavement. For years he was a broken man, and then by the grace of God he succeeded in accepting his son's death, and now he sustains a wonderful medical and Christian ministry. But as you see, it is at the cost of much suffering.

You are clearly called to speak in biblical terms to your patients when they are in your consulting room. Do you ever encounter some reticence on the part of the patient?

You know, I don't talk a lot. I listen. I am sometimes asked if I induce patients to talk about religious matters. That is not at all the case. The doctor's role is to follow the patient, to be ready to accept all the patient has to say—quite the opposite of trying to lead him or give him a lesson in religious knowledge. I have the feeling that I am accompanying my patient. But it is quite a serious undertaking. My patients always end up by coming themselves to essential problems—and it is at that point that most doctors break off the dialog. "That," they will say, "is a matter you must talk to a clergyman about." The doctor is a person to whom one entrusts oneself; he or she ought then to be ready to accompany the patient along all life's detours.

It has happened that ministers and priests have asked me what I do to have so many spiritual conversations with people. I answer that I do nothing. They find people indifferent, but what is really happening is that people tend to defend themselves against anyone who sets out to preach to them. They are always afraid of being hoodwinked, but with a person like me they are not afraid of being hoodwinked. Or else if they are afraid, they say so. I remember a Communist Party leader who in his letter asking for an appointment wrote, "I understand that you are a Christian doctor, and I hope that that will not present any difficulties between us. I will come to consult you on condition that you do not talk to me about questions of religion." I replied that that was understood, and we did some good work together. After the third session, however, I said to him: "I'm very sorry, but I cannot go on."

"How do you mean?"

"Well, I just cannot."

"But why?"

"You made me promise not to touch on religious problems, but you yourself talk about them all the time."

People ask questions, and the search for the meaning of life is not confined to Frankl. The attitude which I recommend is one of being ready to sustain the dialog without breaking it off or running away from it. It is very easy to run away. All you have to do is to ask, "By the way, your mother-in-law—has she got over her bout of flu all right?"—and the dialog is broken off. Broken off on purpose with a neat sidestep. One needs to be really severe with oneself, and to realize that a dialog with a doctor, as with a pastor or priest, is a very serious matter, which one has no right to try and to get out of, and that one must be ready to go along with one's patient right to the end, even if that means into problems of faith or death—so long as those problems are raised by the patient, not by us. It is quite the opposite of the magisterial stance. It is the church's job, not mine, to teach. I teach nobody. I try to accompany people.

My impression is that there is simply not the time to enter into dialog with a patient. One talks of medical matters, but dialog on a spiritual level is almost impossible.

Of course there is some truth in that. Modern life takes us over and everybody complains, but who does anything about it? So, however true that is, we have to realize that we are all responsible; we share a certain complicity in this modern life-style; we do not really give ourselves time any more to meditate, to think, to devote our attention to anybody. We are not just the victims, we are ourselves to blame to some extent. You know, we always find the time to do the things we consider really important. If we are interested in a more profound kind of medicine, in entering into dialog with the patient, we will find the time to do it. And it can happen that a conversation which goes to the root of the matter will actually save an enormous amount of time that would be spent on technical intervention of various kinds, injections, and so on. I am not saying that time is not a problem. In my old age I am having to reduce my activity, and finding it not easy to organize. I have seen lots of people getting into a muddle through not being able to organize their time properly. It is useful for us to ask ourselves if we are making good use of the little time we have, or if we are allowing ourselves to be tossed about like a cork in the torrent of modern life. So there you are! You can turn yourselves into monks in the midst of the turmoil of the world!

I am speaking for several of us in expressing our satisfaction at having been able to read your books, which have been our companions for many years. This evening you have mentioned Kierkegaard and Frankl. But what of Alexis Carrel who was, like you, a doctor, and who worked for so many years at the Rockefeller Institute? In my opinion his book, Man, the Unknown[2] *is far too little known, even though it is a source book for living, written by a Christian doctor and a scientist. We know your books well, but Carrel's work has sunk almost without trace so far as our contemporaries are concerned. Can you suggest why?*

I share your admiration for Carrel. At a certain moment, in 1937, God led me to make a change in my profession, telling me either to abandon it or transform it. I decided to transform it. But how? I meditated on the question. Nelly and I went for a fortnight to the seaside, and I spent the whole time in contemplation, but no word came to me from God. God's silences, you know, are also meant to teach us something. I had only one idea— to reread *Man, the Unknown* and see if there, at the limit of science—Carrel's book was like a summing up of science—there was something that my faith could bring to medicine. Then God said to me, "Start by doing what I have indicated, and I shall give you other ideas afterwards." We are always looking for a grand programme of action, full of great ideas, when the thing is to begin by obeying the little ideas. My little idea was to reread Carrel, and that is what I did.

I believe that what damaged Carrel's reputation was the fact that Marshal Pétain made him his Minister of Health. It was a stroke of genius on Pétain's part, but a great misfortune for Carrel who, with the innocence of the scientist, threw himself enthusiastically into the task, and was compromised. Even now in France people hesitate to mention his name at all. He is one more victim of the politics and the divisions of the war. Practically speaking, that is, I believe, the answer to your question. But we are on our own, and you can enjoy all the verities about which Carrel wrote, including those in his little book of prayer.

Eight

How to Make a Marriage Work

Contribution to a symposium published in the USA, 1982

Nelly and I became engaged in 1920, but we did not announce our engagement until 1923, and we married in 1924. At that time, in our society, one did not have premarital sex, nor did one marry before the man had finished his studies. Customs have changed considerably, but I am not sure that young people today are in general happier than we were.

My wife and I came from the same background; our families were acquainted. Her grandmother had actually been in my father's catechism class, and we had both received our religious instruction from the same pastor, my father's successor at the cathedral. We had gotten to know each other as monitor and monitress in his catechism class.

So of course our desire was to set up a Christian home, which implied, in addition to the evening prayers which I used to say, having a little service together from time to time, just the two of us. As Nelly was shy it was I again who used to read a Bible passage; I knew enough to be able to add a short commentary and a prayer. Basically I was playing at being a pastor and she at being the attentive member of the congregation. But we put no enthusiasm into it. We both felt rather uneasy, so that we felt no urge to continue a ceremony which we felt was no more than a duty.

In any case we got on together very well. Neither of us doubted our mutual love. Nelly had a boundless admiration for me, which I found flattering. She scarcely ever risked contradicting or criticizing me, except on very rare occasions when she did so unexpectedly and explosively, and I put it down to her nervous temperament. Her nervousness I accounted for by the fact that as a child she had been seriously underestimated, being constantly compared with a sister who, unlike her, performed brilliantly at school, and adapted more readily than she to the narrowly conformist outlook of the family.

So I explained all that to her, encouraged her to have more self-confidence, but without realizing that the more I taught her and exhorted her the more I was placing her in a position of inferiority as regards myself. The same happened with her violent outbursts; I tried to remain calm in face of them, and prided myself on doing so, until sometimes I wanted to burst out as well. Then we would both weep, and make it up as Christian husbands and wives ought to do.

Of course such occasions were rare, and we were fairly pleased with our marital success. But basically nothing had been resolved. One day I was talking to an English colleague about another of my doctor friends, and saying how sorry I was for him because his wife was such a nervous person. My English colleague replied by asking me, "Don't you think that if a doctor's wife is very nervous, it is her husband's fault?" I said nothing, but it set me thinking. Could it be that Nelly's nervousness did not come from her childhood, I wondered, but possibly from her present situation? But I did not see myself as in any way responsible.

Now, it was about that time that we were initiated into the practice of the quiet time with God—in 1932, imagine! In a few months time that will make it just a half-century ago! One November evening, at a friend's house, I met some people who had recently joined a movement called the Oxford Group, because it had started among the students of that university, and of which I knew nothing except that it had morally transformed one of my patients who had a very difficult disposition. There were three well-known people from Zurich there and several from Geneva, among them an important official from the League of Nations.

I did not give them a very friendly reception, because I wanted to discuss with them their principles and practices, but they kept on recounting little personal experiences. The official, however, said that for several months he had been devoting a longish period each morning, an hour on average, to being silent and listening to God. That had touched me, because I was very conscious of the poverty of my personal spiritual life when I was so deeply involved in the church.

So, next morning, I got up an hour earlier, quietly so as not to disturb Nelly, and I went into my study, saying to myself, "I want to see what happens if I listen to God for an hour." But the hour passed without my having anything to record. I found it quite possible to construct ideas for sermons in my head, but I knew quite well that what I was looking for was something very different and much more personal. Nevertheless, as I left my study the thought came to me that this was not enough, and I must try again. And with that thought, another: "Well, now! That thought probably comes from God!"

That the God of the Bible is a God who speaks, I was in no doubt. You can see that from the very first page. And God speaks not only to people in general, as when he dictates the law on Sinai, but also in quite personal terms when he sends Moses to speak to Pharaoh, when he awakens the child Samuel, or when he tells Jeremiah to visit the potter. I saw that it was I who did not know how to listen. So I persevered, and gradually I learned to listen; not without making frequent mistakes, to be sure. It is not easy to know whether a thought comes from God. But I learned that the important thing is not never to make mistakes, but rather to approach God so as the better to listen to him.

Two weeks later Nelly and I went to Lyon. We had left home early, and had finished our shopping, and were having lunch. I said shyly to Nelly: "I should like to get home in good time, because I want to do something I wasn't able to do this morning."

"Oh, me too!" she said. "I've started the habit of meditating each morning. The wife of your Dutch friend from the League of Nations suggested it to me."

We had a good laugh at discovering that we had each been hiding from the other the experience to which we had committed ourselves. Naturally we had been waiting to be able to produce some positive results before talking about it.

We decided to try and meditate together on our return home. But what happened was that we experienced the same sense of awkwardness which we had had in our mini services! I found no sense of inner quiet; my emotions spoiled everything, and I finished up without anything worth recording in my notebook. Fortunately Nelly said to me, "We must try again tomorrow and ask God where this awkward feeling comes from." By the next day I was more composed, but I cannot remember what I wrote down. I do however remember, and I shall never forget, what Nelly had written: "You know, you are my teacher, my doctor, my psychologist, even my pastor, but you are not my husband."

She was not making a sexual claim. On that score I was indeed her husband. It was a call for equality. There is no true communion except in equality, and no true equality except before God; not an equality of knowing or doing, but of being, of the person. It is there that we can feel equal, however different we may be from each other. I was an intellectual, Nelly was not; I was an arguer, and ideas broker. And all at once, under God's inspiration, Nelly had put her finger on my problem, which I myself was unaware of. It took me some months to see and understand this, and years to see its full significance—men are so sure of themselves in their masculine rationality in the face of intuition! In my solitude as an orphan I had repressed the emotional side of my nature, and in compensation had exaggerated my intellectualism in order to gain entry into society through the impersonal game of ideas, discussions, and action, because I could not express my real feelings.

Even my religion consisted of ideas about God, about Jesus, about man and salvation—dogma. And as for my wife, I made speeches to her, I gave her lessons in psychology, philosophy, and everything else that could possibly be taught. But my feelings, my anxieties and my despairs, I was unable to talk about. It was all this which came welling up into our long silences: pictures, painful memories, unexpressed regrets, resolutions never kept. It was there that for the first time in my life I wept over the death of my father, and of my mother.

Oh, those early years of quiet times together as man and wife—how they transformed our relationship! I learned to really listen to my wife. We were like confessors to each other, and from then on, in so far as it is possible in this world, we knew each other's most intimate concerns. We told each other in those hours so many things that we should never have said to each other in the rush of daily life. Even couples who are very close unconsciously filter what they say and do not say to each other: many happily married couples have lots of things they never talk about; often for the sake of peace and to avoid conflict. In such cases these things are repressed, and the conflict remains unresolved.

The analogy between religious meditation together with another person and psychoanalysis is obvious. It was Freud who rediscovered, in a nonreligious context, the power of silence and of listening. There are, however, two essential differences: in the case of the psychoanalyst, he remains silent, in particular he offers no observation of his own, whereas in religious meditation there is reciprocity, and in addition the intense seeking after the presence of God which is characteristic of meditation. In the love of God, everything can be said. In psychoanalysis also, it is the analyst's love—a reflection of the love of God, even if he does not know it—which helps the patient to say things he has never before dared to say, and to break through all the filters of self-regard.

So we continued, at least once a week for more than forty years, with our three-cornered rendezvous: God, Nelly, and I. Such a conjugal quiet time complements the personal quiet time, and vice versa. All my subsequent career and activities have been rooted in it. It allowed Nelly fully to share in my vocation, without thereby knowing anything of my patients' problems, for in meditation I am concerned with my own secrets, and not those of other people.

On the occasion of one of the international conferences on the medicine of the whole person, where all the participants knew us well, Dr. Paul Plattner took Nelly and me as an example to illustrate C. G. Jung's teaching on the evolution function of marriage and of the social encounter of the sexes: "Paul," he said, "was once a false intellectual who had repressed his battered affectivity and developed his objectivity. In contact with Nelly he rediscovered his true nature—that sensitivity which has made him the doctor of the whole person that he is. On the other hand, Nelly, who had not liked school, had repressed her intellectual function, and so exaggerated her emotional side. In contact with Paul she began to enjoy using ideas, and she succeeds very well, as you see." It is not only a matter therefore of becoming aware of those subterranean marital problems, of facing them and resolving them in so far as that is possible, but—for each of the partners—of growing, of surpassing oneself so as to attain what Jung calls individuation. And, finally, this effect, which is really the driving force of the whole process, flows from the resolute approach to God by a husband and wife who come together to listen to his voice.

Nine

KNOWING HOW TO GROW OLD

Two interviews on Swiss-French Radio, 1973 and 1974

Doctor, how many important turning points do you consider there are in a person's life?

It is always dangerous to systematize, but since you press me. . . . Really, there are three major periods, namely, childhood, working life, and retirement. Between these three phases there are two turning points. There is the turning point between childhood and adulthood, which has been the subject of intensive study by the psychologists, especially the school of Freud. One must stop being a child in order to become an adult, and it is not so easy to become an adult. Many people run away from it, and remain children all their lives. There is a second turning point between working life and what Jung calls the evening of life. I mention Jung because it is he in particular who has studied this second turning point. The more interesting one's working life has been, the more difficult it is suddenly to reorientate one's existence. Consequently, this turning point between working life and postworking life, which is coming to be known as the third age, is difficult and gives rise to traumas that can be fatal.

In other words, old age begins with retirement?

Yes, but earlier still, you know. In a doctor's eyes one begins to grow old from the first day of life. We spend our lives growing old. The whole of life is a sort of vital capital which one is eating into all the time. One ought to be able imperceptibly to prepare for one stage during the preceding one. For example, we prepare for working life during childhood, and old age ought to be prepared for during our working lives. But people are so absorbed in their work, sometimes so deadened by it, that retirement takes them by surprise. They have not furnished their lives with durable goods which will still be there when their work has gone. That is what preparation for retirement is. It means living in a way which prepares for an old age which will be a broadening of life, an apotheosis of life—the word is Dr. Durckheim's—an apotheosis and not a retraction.

Because basically, before retirement people are conditioned by their work?

Surely!

It is work which gives them meaning?

Surely, surely! You must realize that there are innumerable masses of people who are entirely conditioned by work, by a kind of routine. Each day they catch the train or the bus at the same time, they see the same people, go through the same motions for forty or fifty years; they read only the one paper, even their holidays are packaged. In short, everything tends to crush personal initiative and individual imagination. Especially imagination—it does not do to have too much of that in an organization, or you will find yourself thought of as something of a troublemaker. People are conditioned so that they are diminished, reduced to the status of robots. Then when the moment of liberty comes—and that is after all the goal of human life—they do not know what to do with their liberty.

It is not true that many may even be made to feel ashamed of their liberty?

They are indeed made to feel ashamed of this liberty. Not to be working when others are working, makes them feel they are scroungers, living on the backs of those who are working. This old idea that one is living at others' expense is a constantly recurring theme. The mistress of the house feels ashamed because she is peacefully reading a book while the daily help is sweeping. She looks as if she is doing nothing, whereas the book is probably of considerable cultural value to her. You see it with vacations. Vacations are something quite new. For a long time they were the privilege of a quite small section of the population. Now they are general; they are a right. There are established holidays, and yet people feel a need to justify themselves for going on vacation. They say, "Ah, I've been feeling so tired recently," as if to say, "You know, I have a right to this privilege." They are trying to excuse themselves for a kind of disobedience to the law of work. Work has become the purpose of human existence.

It is possibly also a way of having an existence. Don't you think that we exist through our work, through our action?

There you touch on a problem which has concerned me for a long time, and which is very profound, namely the need to have meaning for one's life, and the need to feel that one really exists, even. I do not want to digress from our subject, but I have just been talking to a woman who said to me, "It is my pain which makes me feel that I really exist." That is probably a less uncommon sentiment than we realize. People have even been known to seek particular forms of suffering because that is the way they are enabled to feel that they exist. This feeling of existing or not existing touches on the problem that besets the existentialist philosophers. We must not let ourselves be led off on that particular sidetrack, but it is closely connected with the problem you have raised, because if human beings exist through their work, then when their work is taken away they have a feeling of emptiness, of nonexistence, and even feel the need to justify their existence, perhaps through bad temper or endless grumbling.

In relation to society, then, human beings exist by virtue of their work?

Yes, of course, of course! It was not so in ancient Greece, for example. There, of course, there was the problem of slavery. But in their cities, men argued in the agora, and they had the feeling that they existed because they faced life's problems, and not because they contributed to the material prosperity of their society.

So, when you are conditioned, say by forty years of work, it is in the end very difficult to go over into retirement, is it not?

It is very difficult—and then there is work and work. There is for instance the work of a doctor: it is a perpetual adventure. It is something which necessarily involves our thought, our education. We have to keep up with the times; it is something which continually develops us. But assembly-line work in a factory, where all you have to do is tighten the same bolt in the same component as it passes under your nose—I assure you that it diminishes people, and in the end turns them into veritable robots. So there has been a tendency, for reasons of economy and profit, to reduce people to the status of servants of machines. It is absolutely essential that society should change its concept of work, and understand that the true meaning of work is to be found in personal development, in the personal contribution which a person makes to society through activity as an individual.

In order to make a success of old age, at what age do you consider one should start thinking about it?

I should say at about forty or fifty.

Some people claim that it is necessary to start thinking about it as early as adolescence.

Yes; I set a limit on it in order not to fall into paradox. For example, a sociologist questioned a young woman of eighteen: "What do you think about your old age?" She replied, "I hope to die before then." It is a quite natural response for an eighteen-year-old. One cannot ask children. . . . Their job is to prepare for active life, not for old age, and yet they are already preparing themselves for it by the way they enter upon their lives. If they look upon life as an adventure, if they look upon it as a commitment, well, they are preparing for a happy old age, because old age is the fruit of the life one has lived. It is like a sort of moment of truth in which is revealed either the plenitude that is within us, or else the void, if we suddenly realize that the motive force of

our life has been removed. It was external to us, in work
routines or in family goals which are no longer there
when retirement comes. For example, for a woman there
is a kind of retirement at the moment when her last child
marries, and her own task as a mother—her professional
task as a mother—comes to an end. That often repre-
sents a difficult crisis for a woman, who then attaches
herself to her grandchildren, and enters into conflict
with her daughters-in-law.

*In other words, if I have understood you correctly, in order
to prepare for old age, and to try and make a success of it,
the first thing is to give one's life meaning.*

Or find meaning in one's life. The difference is an important one. Because, basically, it is not we who provide
the meaning. Take two old people. One has manifestly
made a success of old age, and the other has made a
mess of it. Well, it is not a matter of merit or blame, in
either case. Those who make a success of their lives do
so not because they have prepared themselves properly
for it; and those who make a success of old age do so
not because they have prepared for it. It is because they
have lived with a meaning to their lives, a meaning
which will go on into old age. As for the others, it is
not their fault if society has conditioned them, has am-
putated any creative imagination there may have been
in them. Making speeches at them is not going to convince them that something else is required. What we
have to do is to undertake the task of changing society,
changing the concept of work and even of human beings
themselves. A society which gives a meaning to people's
lives must be a better society than one which removes
all meaning, which is inhuman because it takes away
the meaning of life. The best things in life come to us

without our having manufactured them, you know—
even if it is only a daisy plucked by the roadside.

*Do you not think, doctor, that the basis of proper
preparation for old age is to be found in our standard of
education? In our system, call it our capitalist structure, we
have to recognize that a good education is a class-based
privilege. Don't you think it is an essential prerequisite for
the successful old age and retirement of which you speak?*

I quite agree with you when you say that it is a class-
based privilege. A doctor who has been the confidant
of so many people is well aware of that. And yet there
are people from the underprivileged classes who have
a sense of culture, and develop it all their lives. They
are very special people, who, swimming against the current of an inhumane society, show a kind of need to
develop themselves, to find out more about the world,
a need to enrich their own personalities. That is real
education, the enrichment of the personality, the enrichment of a person's relationship with the world.
Those who have that gift, even if they come from an
underprivileged background, succeed in breaking
through the ceiling of inhumanity set by our society,
and enjoy a happy old age because it is for them a pro-
gression, not a regression. But some training is required.
A man who has been so immersed in his work that he
has not even had the time to read a book, but just
glanced through magazines, comes to his retirement,
and what happens? He is completely at a loose end. You
suggest to him that he should take up reading—a good
book is a wonderful companion. He goes and gets one;
he reads a page; but he has so got out of the habit of
reading that he puts it down and goes back to being
bored, rather as in the past he used to go back to his
office.

It is possible that he has not taken up reading or any form of cultural activity during his working life because his job was too exhausting? When one does an eight-hour shift down a mine or in a factory, one is possibly too tired for self-education in the evening.

Yes, of course. . . . That depends on the conditions in which we find ourselves; it depends a little, too, on our own disposition. There are people who have the gift, even when surrounded by apparently uninteresting things, always to be learning something. Others learn nothing, even if they travel round the world. They are wealthy enough to go anywhere for their vacations, and they come back just as intellectually and spiritually poverty-stricken as when they set out. They have learned nothing, while there are others who are always learning something new, even from snatches of conversation, from a TV program, or what have you. An enormously important role is played, in making a success of old age, by that spirit of curiosity and adventure.

Obviously I am using the term culture in a restricted sense, because culture covers such a very vast field—in one sense it is the way we react to things.

Yes, we have a prejudice towards too intellectual a view, haven't we? Our schooling sets its stamp on our idea of culture. Jung said that the culture imparted by the school is a standard culture, which turns out people according to a mold which is designed primarily with social success—and that means job success—in view. True education, true culture, is something much more personal. As the recipient of people's confidences, I am astonished at the number of people who manage to educate themselves—clandestinely, you might say. They think themselves uncultured because they don't have a degree of some sort, whereas they are much more cultured than they imagine, and are often really rich personalities. All art belongs to culture, and all philosophy. And there is a philosophy which is not confined to the philosophers: it is a philosophy of life, that is to say, a search for the meaning of life, a thirst for life, which is one of the characteristics of true culture.

And you think that this culture, in the very wide sense of the term, is absolutely indispensable for a happy retirement, or should we say a happy old age, and that it does in fact make it possible to fill in the chasm which exists at the age of sixty-five between work and retirement?

The importance of continuing education is beginning to be understood, and I believe that in the future we shall see further developments in that direction. One sees increasing attention paid to recreational evening classes and adult education. The idea has gone that childhood alone is the proper time for study. It is beginning to be realized that one can go on studying throughout one's life, and that studying is not just accumulating knowledge, but discovering a relationship with the world, both practically and intellectually. The retired person who has a little workshop, where he practices DIY, has a relationship with the world as he uses his machines—as he uses his hands. That is culture, just as surely as that of the philosopher who studies Socrates or Descartes.

And you yourself, doctor, you are seventy-five. Do you have the feeling that old age, if you put its beginning at, say, sixty-five, is still a time of progress? For you, has it meant progress?

For me old age has to be a time of progress, and I recognize that I am highly privileged. On the one hand because I am a doctor, and doctors can go on. They don't have a strict retiring age like office workers, but they are exceptionally privileged. On the other, because I have several strings to my bow: I am not only a doctor, but also a writer, and a social worker, and I am in the midst of an adventure at this moment. You only need to write a book on old age for people to bombard you with all kinds of social activities. I feel that that is carrying me off into a new adventure. But if it weren't that, it would be something else. In other words, we must always be multi-purpose. We must retain the capacity to adapt ourselves to new things, so that new faculties, new elements can be developed when we have more time on our hands, so that we can use the liberty that retirement gives us for something other than purely gainful, productive work.

You feel you are still very much integrated into our society?

Oh, yes, yes! Only, I am an exception. I must recognize that. I am a privileged person. I am asked to write a book on retirement. I am the right age, but I don't have the right conditions. Nobody has cut me off from my work. I can organize my life as I wish—and that is always difficult to do, mind you! I always have more requests than I can accede to, but that has always been the case.

On the basis of conversations you have had with your patients, both men and women, do you have the feeling that old people are rather despised, or that they feel despised?

That is because of the prejudice of society which values a person in terms of productivity. There is a kind of prejudice which disparages old age, against which we must fight tooth and nail, because human beings are not validated by work; it is work which has its value because it comes from human beings. We see some people who, on their retirement, suddenly seem to blossom and find new activities. I have known numerous examples among my own patients. Some, who were afraid of retirement, have suddenly seen that it presents the possibility of new human horizons, with limitations, of course. What does not have its limitations in this world? But it has the capability of offering much fuller life than the a working life that precedes it, which is often a form of slavery.

Don't you think that the idea of nonproductivity is peculiarly a Western notion? In Japan, for example, it is absent; in fact the old person is admired and respected.

In Black Africa, too. And in the ancient world. So it is a pure prejudice arising out of the Industrial Revolution. On both sides! On the Marxist side as well as the capitalist, work has been glorified and turned into a sort of modern deity; a Moloch of a god, which devours people.

We ought to be glorifying dreams now, or idleness.

You know, in May '68, when the demonstrating students wrote "Up with imagination!" it was the sign of a need to react against a rationalistic society which prizes only one thing, productivity. I do not repudiate it, because it has brought us prosperity, and without that prosperity there would be no retirement at all. Retirement is not such a long-established institution. The aim, therefore, is not to smash the machine, but to liberate men and women. It was an American writer, David Riesman, who asked the question: prosperity, yes, but what for? In other words, is there a purpose for this society, well-organized as it is, which nevertheless devours its own children? The only possible purpose is the development of the person, and that development is not work, but one's soul, one's innermost self.

Thank you, doctor.

* * *

In this evening's Medical Magazine our guest is a person of considerable stature: Dr. Paul Tournier, Genevan, writer, specialist in old age and old people, particularly well known in the United States, where an important book has just been published in his honor, containing contributions from some forty doctors, scientists, sociologists, and philosophers. At seventy-six he could not be better placed to talk about old people and old age. Dr. Tournier, who are these old people whose lives you know and share?

To be aged is not to cease to be a person, invested with all the dignity proper to the human person. The old have not shed their humanity.

So being old is much more a state than an illness.

It is not an illness. You could as well ask if youth is an illness, on the grounds that there are childhood illnesses. Obviously there are old people who are ill; and they run a greater risk of sickness or infirmity. Failing hearing, failing sight, play a large role in the lives of old people. These are medical matters, and it is our job to treat disease. The problem you are asking me about is old age, and old age is not a disease, it is one of the phases of life. There is a childhood phase, an adult phase, and as for what follows, people think, "We'll see later on." They remove from their horizon this last phase, old age. We simply must reintegrate it into life, so that old people may feel that they really are a part of life, full fellow-citizens of the living.

*But who ought then to be doing the training for old age—
the aged themselves, particular old people with power and
influence, or society in general? At the present time it seems
that there is no real well-understood contact between youth
and age, or between the generations.*

Yes, and it derives from a certain social prejudice, a tendency to segregate old people. When people speak in a
somewhat patronizing tone to old people—"There,
there, not to worry . . ."—in the way children are spoken to, they are in fact depriving them of their sense of
being part of the reality of the human race. Social prejudice against old people makes them hide themselves
away. It's a sort of apartheid. They hide at the back of
the public bar, playing cards. They are quite cut off. Go
into any restaurant and you will see them huddled together in the darkest corner. There is no contact between
them and the other people who have just come in from
their place of work, who have lots to talk about, who
are still part of life. They are outside life. In any bar you
can see the frontier between the old folks' territory and
the territory of those who are still alive. It is absolutely
necessary—and people are beginning to realize it—it is
necessary to bring about the reintegration of the old into
everyday life. That is why we must vigorously strive for
the establishment, one by one, of a network, a tapestry
of relations between the young and the old.

*But who ought to be making the effort, the old person, or
the young?*

I was asked to write a book about old people, but what
I did was to write some chapters addressed to the young,
and I said to them: "Get to know old people. You have
a lot to learn from them." At one time the aged used to

remain within the family. Now, with changes in life-style, with smaller dwellings, there are large numbers of children who you might say do not know any old people. That leaves a gap in their education, in their personal upbringing. The grandmother who in the past used to recount old legends and sing songs to her grand-children is something that is tending to disappear. The old man is put in a home, and the child is then taken to pay a visit to grandpa. They have nothing to say to each other; a piece of barley-sugar is presented, and the visit is over. There is no true dialog, whereas in reality there is a tremendous affinity between the young and the old. At the age of eighteen one argues about the meaning of life, one argues passionately and one criti-cizes one's parents. One says, "Anyway, I have no in-tention of slaving away all my life like my parents, never having a minute to myself. Life oughtn't to be like that. Honestly, my parents have never lived. They've been the slaves of work." And those are the young people who declare, "I'm just not going to live a life like that." Perhaps they will become hippies and take themselves off to Afghanistan, though the ones that do that are a very small number. All these young people who argue so passionately about whether life has any meaning— well, they get married, they take up apprenticeships, and they are caught willy-nilly in the toils of the life they have been arguing against. And it makes them into ro-bots in their turn. They have their troubles, their chil-dren fall ill, rivals at work get on their nerves. So there is a whole stage when one is caught in a life that seems pointless—you understand my meaning: a life that has no meaning. Go and ask someone who is like that, in mid-career, whether he thinks life has a meaning. He will tell you, "That's a question for the philosophers. I've no time for such things. I've got enough on my hands with my responsibilities and worries about my job, and about the family as well. The meaning of life—really you ought to ask someone who has nothing better to do." Then they reach their retirement, and all at once they think about their lives: "Does it all have a meaning? Isn't it just like a machine that keeps on turning round and round? Isn't it society that treats us as puppets and makes up our lives for us?" At the very point where they are beginning to have some freedom, they have no idea what to do with it.

Is what you are saying, then, that we have to learn to grow old?

Yes, but you must start in good time. That is why people are beginning to think about preparation for old age. The idea is gaining ground. A start has been made especially in the United States, and it is beginning to take on in Europe. I get requests nowadays from all kinds of sources, and particularly from commerce and industry. There are firms now which take the trouble to gather together those who are approaching retirement—but even if it covers the last five years before retirement, that is already rather late. But of course most people put off thinking about it until "later on." And later on, it is too late, at least for a lot of people. Naturally it depends on the individual person. There are some to whom a passion for collecting butterflies or postage stamps is going to be an enormous help in enabling them to slip smoothly into a rich old age; but those whose only interest in life has been their job may face a crisis which can be fatal. An enormous number of people die soon after retiring, and they are the very ones who have been the best workers, who have devoted themselves exclusively to their jobs. We have got to realize that life is something more than one's job.

Does that mean that to sit back and take things easy, upon retirement is harmful for the old person?

Taking things easy is more harmful for old people than for the young.

Nevertheless the popular saying is: "He really does deserve to take things easy."

Yes of course—we read about those sociological enquiries: the sociologist goes into old people's homes, finds people bored from morning till night, and asks the question: "Wouldn't you like to find something to occupy your time?" The reply comes: "I've slaved away all my life, so I reckon I have a right to rest now." The idea has got through that retirement means rest. But it need not mean rest, it can mean the chance to construct a life based on things one likes doing, on one's interests, on one's own drive and inspiration; a life of freedom in place of life amid the shackles of work . . . . That is why I have suggested the expression "a second career." There is room in the lives of every one of us for a second career, and one may say that the most successful lives are those in which a person, after retiring, has been able to pursue something—and I don't mean merely a hobby like fishing, because that can be just a way of killing time. Something more is needed, something that enthrals—even if it is only a stamp collection. Learning a language, for example: it is quite possible to learn a language over a few years; and it isn't just the language, there is the literature, the encounter with a different way of thinking, and so on. Only, all of this requires you to take the initiative, it needs imagination, which is what society kills. You know how imaginative and inventive a child is. Children transfigure everything that comes to hand. It can be whatever they want: a soldier. . . . Then the whole of life sets to work eroding that imagination. Even at school, if they dream, they get their knuckles rapped—they're bad pupils. The good pupils are the ones who attend only to what they are told to do. Later, in a job, the good employees are the ones who spend no time dreaming about what they will do on Sunday, but get on with their work.

We saw just now that old age was a state and in no sense a disease, but in that state, what does the aged person himself think? Does he regret his married life, for instance?

There are old people who are turned backwards. They think only about their past, either to idealize it, talk about it (adjusting it here and there), or else to complain: "What might I not have done if they hadn't spoiled my life?" It is always other people's fault. On the other hand, the direction of real living is always forwards. The old people who are happy are the ones who have a plan for tomorrow, not those who are always thinking of what they were doing thirty years ago.

But learning to grow old, is that not also learning to die?

Death is also the future. We must remove death from the taboo that surrounds it. In civilizations in which death is better understood as the most personal thing in life—for example among the Japanese, and also the antiquity—this kind of taboo on death is attenuated, and death is treated in a more natural way. Perhaps it is the price we have to pay for medical progress. People have come to believe that they have a right to health. They almost end up thinking they have a right not to die. The deep awareness that life involves death, that death is part and parcel of life. . . . I have an American colleague, actually she is a Swiss, Dr. Elisabeth Kübler-Ross, who has taken upon herself the task of talking to people who are dying. It's quite a moving story. She went to a hospital and asked to talk to people who were dying. She got the answer, "There aren't any." She realized how strong was the wish not to seem to have any. In the end she found them, and she conducted hundreds of interviews with the dying. All of them were beset by anxieties about which they talked to no one. Reading Dr. Kübler-Ross's story is a moving experience. It is overwhelming. It is also commonplace. It is impressive because it is so commonplace. She approaches a dying man. His wife says to her: "He has cancer. But we haven't told him. He couldn't bear it."

She goes calmly up to him and says: "Are you seriously ill?"

"Oh, I've got cancer." As simple as that. He feels tremendous relief at being able to say it, to say what he is thinking.

She says to him: "But what is it you are afraid of?"

"I just hope that my children will miss me a bit."

It sounds so very commonplace; yet most people die in spiritual isolation.

What about religion?

Religion? I think it is better to start early than to leave it to the last moment. It's a bit like everything else, isn't it? There is a saying: "The devil was sick, the devil a monk would be." We tend to think of religion as a sort of final consolation, when there is no further human hope. But true religion is living our whole lives with God. It means binding ourselves to God even as children, and living our family lives, our working lives, our social lives, with God. That gives a meaning to life, and it will go on and develop more and more right into old age.

All that, of course, forms part of the apprenticeship for old age, the philosophy of old age, which is your own experience. But do you yourself, personally, have a recipe for your own enthusiasm at the age of seventy-six?

I have frequently had to make fresh starts in my life. We too easily become the slaves of routine, you understand, and the great enemy of life is routine. Routine clogs you, it ossifies you. At various points in my life I have made a succession of fresh starts, conversions, first in the way of social work, then in the way of a living Christian faith, and then in the way of integrating that into medicine. I have been the prime mover in a whole movement in medicine, and now the time has come when I have no longer to lead it. The leadership has to be left to younger people, and they have taken over. I play the kindly grandfather who comes along to pass the time of day with them—but I think I can say that I am still the darling granddad of the movement! And now I am asked to produce a book on old age, and that opens the gates to a flood of speaking engagements. It is one more fresh start for me. My career as a speaker, like my career as a writer, has come along to renew my life. I have written a book on the adventure of living.[1] I do not think any adventure lasts. We should always like to make them last, when really we ought always to be starting on a new adventure. What I should like to do is to say to the old, "A new adventure is opening out before you, it's up to you to enter into it."

Ten

WHAT IS ESSENTIAL IN MY LIFE

Contribution to a symposium published in German, 1983

I think the most important event in my life was the death of my mother. My father was already dead: he was seventy when I was born, and died two months later. A babe in arms has no awareness of his father's death. He gradually gets to know the people around him; that one is missing he neither knows nor feels. It is difficult, of course, in the case of the death of the mother, as happened with Jean-Jacques Rousseau, because of the unique bond existing between the newborn child and his mother.

I can well imagine the closeness of the bond between my mother and me, how attached she must have been to me, how she must have cherished the little baby boy whom her aged and revered husband left to her. For her I was not the Oedipean rival of my father, but his incarnation.

My mother, however, soon fell seriously ill, and had to undergo a series of operations. I was six years old when she died. This time, the shock was profound. I retain scarcely any reminiscences of my mother, whereas people's memories generally go back to the age of four or even further. I can just see myself going up to her sickbed, as if in a fog. Clearly, my memories of her have been suppressed into my unconscious under the pressure of the emotion of her death. I do have a clear memory of being taken with my sister to the home of the uncle and aunt who were to bring us up, and asking, "Sha'n't we ever go back to Mummy's house?"

I wanted for nothing. My uncle and aunt were models of generosity, care, and affection. It was in me that the break had occurred. It was as if I had brought down an iron curtain to protect my wounded heart. I immersed myself in a persistent spiritual solitude. I was shy, shut in upon myself, unable to relate to other children. I have often quoted the word of Dr. Pierre Rentchnick on the psychology of orphans. When he asked me, "What did you feel when your mother died?" I at once replied, "I had the feeling that I did not exist for anyone."

Not to exist means having no rights. I felt I had no right to anything that was done for me. I was the debtor in everything. Even now I find it extremely difficult to ask a favor, to accept a gift. But it has had the effect of making me resourceful, self-sufficient, and ingenious at getting myself out of difficulties, both in practical and in spiritual matters. Despite having written a lot of books, I am not an intellectual, I am a manual worker. My greatest pleasure is in achieving something with my hands.

But this early confrontation with death has made me take life seriously. It is very obvious that people constantly seek to banish the thought of death from their minds, to forget it—at least in our Western civilization. With me, death seems always to have been present, even when I was not expressly thinking about it. I certainly felt this on the death of my wife, eight years ago: I realized that I had already spent my whole life in mourning, waiting to rejoin my parents in heaven. From then on I had one more link with the beyond, one more beloved being waiting for me there. I think that is what makes widowerhood easier for me than it is for many.

That is probably why it was possible for Nelly and me to talk to each other quite simply and frankly about death, right up to the last moment. We were in Athens, where I was lecturing to some Americans. She had suffered a coronary thrombosis, and had been in the hospital for a month, a month that was for us a time of supreme intimacy, in a foreign country as we were. She knew how seriously ill she was. The cardiology specialist had invited me one day to his home in order to tell me, and I had at once discussed it with her.

She knew she was threatened with a second coronary, and that she would be left seriously handicapped, if she did not die. So it was on the last day she suddenly said to me: "Perhaps it would have been better if I had died of my heart attack a month ago."

"And yet my Greek colleagues have done a good job. They saved your life. You are glad of that," I replied.

"Yes, of course, if I can get back to Geneva and see my children and grandchildren." She was silent for a moment, and then added, "But if I had died, I should be in heaven now, and I should be meeting your parents."

I found her remark infinitely touching. You see, she had also married my expectation of heaven!

I replied: "Well, when you arrive in heaven, my parents will thank you for having been the wife that you have been for their son."

It was the last thing I said to her. A moment later she put her hand on her heart and exclaimed, "That's it!"

"Are you sure?"

"Yes."

And she died.

Well, this confrontation with death that I had sensed since childhood has set the direction for my whole life. I think it was instrumental in leading me to two successive decisions at about the age of twelve or thirteen. The first: I said, in private, entirely on my own, "Lord Jesus, I dedicate my life to you." Of course I did not fully realize the significance of that—and I said nothing about it to anyone. But Jesus took that naive child's prayer seriously. He took me by the hand and gradually led me to an understanding of what that dedication meant.

Nor did I know in any precise way why I had made that decision. But what other response is there to the reality of death, than identification with the resurrected Lord? My second decision confirmed the point; it was my choice of vocation. The only subject in which I did well at school was mathematics. But I said to myself, "One mathematician more or less will not make much difference to the sufferings of the world. I want to follow a vocation of service to others; I want to be a doctor." Of course I realize now that a mathematician is as useful to the world as a doctor. But the thing that counted, in my simplicity, was the idea of service.

It was much later, when I had learned something of psychology, that I saw that my decision to become a doctor was a need to compensate for the death of my parents, a means of getting my own back on death by pitting myself throughout my life against it and its depredations among the living. And now, thirty years later, I may have become a writer, but I have not changed my vocation. I do not write for the sake of writing, but in order to continue caring for men and women, to help them to live better lives, to overcome or accept their sufferings.

These two decisions gave my life its meaning. Their mutual interaction too has been significant, since I have been led to an enthusiastic interest in a medicine of the person, an omnidirectional medicine, so to speak, an effort to relieve at once all human sufferings, both physical and spiritual, to unite in a practical way the faith we receive from God and the science we are taught at the university.

But for that I myself needed to be liberated, partially at least, from my complex as an uncommunicative and unsociable orphan. My rescue took place in two stages. First there was my classics teacher—I was sixteen by then—who realized that what this odd child lacked was the experience of relationship with others. He invited me to his home, not as a pupil to receive a lesson, but for a dialog as man to man.

All at once I existed for him, not as a pupil to be taught Greek, but as a person. The result was remarkable. I soon discovered that my intellectual life provided a door through which I could enter into relationship with others, through the exchange of ideas and through argument. This made it possible for me not only to complete my medical studies but also to launch out into social life, to interest myself in all sorts of things—the theatre, literature, law, politics, and student affairs. It was the period of the First World War, and of the Russian revolution, when the optimism of the nineteenth century was crumbling—you can imagine how much there was to discuss! There was work to do as well, for the International Red Cross, Children's Aid, and of course the church.

A second stage was needed, however. I was quite good at speaking in public; I was much less happy in private conversation. As I came away one evening from a student gathering, a friend said to me, "I've just realized that you were an orphan." Suddenly there was a lump in my throat; I could say nothing; I was on the verge of tears. I just ran off into the night! The fact was that the only door to relationship with others that had opened for me was an intellectual one. The way to affective, emotional relationships remained blocked. Intellectual, objective, scientific relationships pertain to the masculine side of human nature; the rest to the feminine side. I was liberated from the death of my father, but not from that of my mother, and I did not know it.

Even within the church all I did was to argue about ideas, dogma, principles and concepts, and join in controversies between orthodoxy and liberalism. I felt acutely the contrast between my ecclesiastical activity and my personal piety. All my resolutions were of no avail; I did not know how to pray. Even with my wife, whom I loved dearly and with whom I got on well, I lectured her, taught her all sorts of facts, but as for expressing my feelings and emotions, I was incapable, as many men are, of doing so—such things are, in fact, what interest women.

When we began sharing our quiet time together, she dared to say to me, "You are my teacher, my doctor, my psychologist, my pastor, but you are not my husband." She had put her finger neatly on my problem. Ideas are like the change that passes from one person's pocket to another's: a thing, impersonal. What commits us personally is feeling, the life of the emotions.

The practice of meditation transformed my relationship, not only with my wife, but with other people generally, and notably with my patients. I had been in general practice for eight years, and reckoned I knew them well enough. And all at once here they were telling me secrets that they had never trusted me with before, because now they felt intuitively that I was interested in them as persons and not just as cases.

We had come across a religious movement which was called the Oxford Group, because it had started among the students of that university. It advocated complete openness between individuals about all those things that worry us and which we habitually conceal. I was a keen and militant member of the movement for almost fifteen years. As I was a doctor, people were ready to open their hearts to me, and I became more and more aware of how lonely they were with their heavy secrets, and of the considerable part that all these problems played in their physical and psychic health.

We discover our real problems when we are silent before God, listening to his voice. Of course, I have often made mistakes—it is easy to imagine that one's own thoughts are the authentic voice of God. But in fact what happens is that with practice in meditation one comes to recognize one's mistakes. One learns to become more honest with oneself. Freud, in a completely nonreligious context, spoke of the power that silence had in this respect. So that my own experience was quite close to that of the psychoanalysts. One day in 1937 I saw that I ought to devote myself entirely to this field of research. This time I believe I was not mistaken, and that the call was from God.

However, on the eve of the Second World War the founder of the movement, Dr. Frank Buchman, sensing the approaching conflict, changed both the name and the orientation of the movement, making it a more structured, more homogeneous, more disciplined force, aimed at exerting a more effective influence on the destiny of the world. It was after the war, in 1946, that I saw how divergent our paths were becoming. I had to break away from my friends, whose talk was of enrollment, ideology, and strategy—objectives far removed from my vocation of helping individuals in their free search for their own inner calling.

The separation was very painful, despite the emotional and spiritual bonds that subsisted between us. But it was just then that I found myself being approached by doctors from various countries who shared my concern. They had read my first book, *Médecine de la personne*, which had been published during the war, in 1940. This idea of a medicine which addresses itself to man in his irreducible unity and in his physical, psychological, social, and spiritual totality, had awakened in them a lively response, and they wished to study it further with me.

Again, it was about that time that I was invited to go to Germany to work in the Evangelical Academy of Bad Boll, which had just been founded. Germany was then the scene of material and moral ruin. There was a realization that the reason why Nazism had been able to plunge the country into such a frightful adventure, and to use, for example, both law and medicine in assaults on human dignity of the worst possible kind, was because those disciplines had long been divorced from their spiritual sources in our civilization.

Everything had to be called in question so as to rediscover the true meaning of culture. Those years of passionate discussions in a ruined Germany, with doctors, lawyers, artists, economists, and architects, had a decisive influence upon me. Thereafter I continued and enlarged them in my own field of medicine, with colleagues of every sort of speciality, from different countries and belonging to different religious denominations.

Together we started the Bossey Group, so named because we held our first sessions in the Chateau de Bossey, the headquarters of the Ecumenical Institute near Geneva.

Medicine is not just a scientific and technological matter; it has a human dimension as well. It uses science and technology in its fight against disease, but through a personal relationship with a patient the doctor also helps the patient to become a person in the full sense of the term, not only in his or her individual development, but also in harmonious relationship with nature, with fellow human beings, and with God.

All these questions, raised both in these international conferences and in so many years of daily medical practice, led me to my career as a writer and lecturer.

So we can see a connected sequence of events in our lives, and it seems a most interesting idea of Dr. Hans Schaffner to invite old people such as myself to discover and reveal what is the essential ingredient that has determined the way their lives had developed. In doing so I have necessarily oversimplified, but it does seem to me that my mother's death is the silken thread that leads to an understanding of the sort of person I am. My mother's death, my great misfortune. Of course it is not that it was the cause of the way my life unfolded: many orphans remain shattered throughout their lives by the traumas of childhood.

We have little control over the events of our lives, whether good or bad. What we are responsible for is our reaction to those events, either positive or negative. But we are not alone responsible, because our reaction depends on the help that others give us. That help from others always arises out of true personal encounters, which are really quite rare. I think it is always the grace of God which inspires a person to make the move towards that true encounter, just at the moment it is needed to lead us through our sorrows or our joys, our failures and our successes. What is left in the evening of our life, except what has come from God?